Graye

BOOKS BY DEBORAH FLETCHER MELLO

MaGregor Press

Rested Waters

Harlequin Kimani Romance

Passionate Premiere
Forever A Stallion
Seduced By A Stallion
Promises To A Stallion
Lost In A Stallion's Arms
Tame A Wild Stallion
To Love A Stallion
Always Means Forever
In The Light of Love

Harlequin Kimani Arabesque

Forever And A Day
The Right Side of Love
A Love For All Time
Take Me To Heart

Graye

A NOVEL

BY

Deborah Fletcher Mello

MaGREGOR PRESS

This is a work of fiction. All names, characters, places, incidents and dialogue, are either the product of the author's imagination or are used fictitiously, and any resemblance to actual persons, living or dead, business establishments, events or locales is entirely coincidental.

Published by MaGregor Press

ISBN-13: 978-0615705934
ISBN-10: 0615705936

Graye

Printed in the United States of America
First printing, October 2012
Designed by Doris Arnold - Enduring Graphics

In Memory of My Beloved Grandmother,
Susie M. Cole

A man is born into this world with only a tiny spark of goodness in him.

The spark is God, it is the soul: The rest is ugliness and evil, a shell...

Chaim Potok,
The Chosen

ONE

Jack Daniel's shot that man. Jack Daniel's put the gun in Graye McAdams' hand and pulled the trigger. Graye had tried to make them understand that it had not been him who'd killed Tate Butler, but the bitter of Jack Daniel's running through his bloodstream. Since Graye had spent the better part of his thirty-eight years blaming everything and everyone else for all his ills, it came as no surprise to anyone that he would blame the drink for his putting an end to another man's life.

The sky had gone dark just before the first shot was fired across the back yard, the luminous moon dropping behind a cascade of caliginous clouds. Foreboding is what the old people would later say about it. The McAdams family had been celebrating Miss Jen Pearl's seventieth birthday. Her oldest son, Treat, had hired a band, Walter Wiley and the Nasty Boys. All the McAdams kin, plus the whole neighborhood had gathered together. The mimeographed invitations had read bring your own bottle, so many sat drinking from dark flasks wrapped in brown paper bags while eating Nana Leah's fried chicken and potato salad. One of the cousins had been frying fresh croakers over a gas bayou cooker, keeping a watchful eye on the cornmeal battered fillets. Couples were sweating in the summer heat, shaking large derrieres in flamboyant gyrations to the music. People had come and gone most of the evening, no one restricted to any set time. The party had started early and would have gone well into the morning had Graye not upset the balance of the evening.

Nana Leah would later say she smelled trouble the minute Graye and Angelette arrived, his eyes already heavily glazed. Angelette had been more reserved than usual, cautiously raising her eyes to greet anyone who spoke to her. Graye had clutched her elbow tightly pulling her along beside him, afraid to let go. It had been Graye's obsession with not letting Angelette go that had gotten the best of him.

Standing at the edge of the back porch the two had stood quietly. In a dark silence they observed the goings on, only speaking when spoken to. Every so often Graye would respond to a question or comment, mumbling his words so badly that no one understood him. Angelette did not speak at all, not even when

Tate Butler came bounding down the back steps. Tate had spoken though, extending his hand toward Graye as he did. Graye had only nodded his head not even bothering to look the other man in the eyes until Tate leaned to kiss Angelette gently on the cheek. It was only then that Graye's shoulders lifted and his stance widened. Angelette had blushed profusely, easing her body closer to Graye's, noting the sudden tension spreading through the man's large frame. Her eyes met Tate's only briefly before she'd dropped them back down to the ground.

She listened intently as Tate struck up a conversation, the two men making small talk about the weather, Graye's last fishing trip, and the happenings down at the Easy-Slide Café. Tate had eased himself over to the dance area after that and was doing a nasty grind with some skinny woman in a brown floral dress. Both Angelette and Graye had watched as Tate and the skinny woman wrapped themselves around each other in a seductive twist.

Angelette had dropped a hesitant hand against Graye's arm, slowly caressing his warm flesh and when he'd not pulled away she'd relaxed ever so slightly. Any other time, if another man had smiled, spoken, or acknowledged her presence in a way that did not sit well with Graye, it would have been a nasty fight that would have left her in tears and the tidiness of their home in shambles. Angelette wished a prayer that this night would be different.

No one paid much attention to them after that, not bothering to notice that Graye had polished off a fifth of Jack Daniel's by his lonesome and was starting on his second. Angelette had noticed though as she gently urged her husband to extend their good-byes and head across the street for home. Graye had not budged though, still standing like stone at the bottom of the steps. And then the clouds crossed in front of the moon.

"What you staring at my woman fo'," Graye had shouted sloppily, dropping the bottle in his hand to the ground. Everyone turned to look first toward Graye and the broken shards of glass at his feet and then toward where he stared, his gaze locked on Tate Butler's face, the stainless steel .357 Magnum in his hand aimed at the man's heart. Tate turned his body ever so slightly, his posture tensing. The skinny woman rose from the seat at Tate's side, tripping in drunken stupor over her own two feet as she maneuvered to get herself out of the way. In the distance someone else laughed, a nervous giggle that suddenly seemed as out of place as the hum of the band's equipment. Every inch of sound seemed out of place for the blanket of quiet that had been laid over them all.

Tate eased his hands into the air above his shoulders, his palms raised toward the sky. "We don't have any problems here, Graye," he said softly, his tone even and controlled. "I didn't mean you any disrespect. Put the gun away, Gray," he intoned.

Graye staggered slightly. Angelette whispered his name into the darkness, her tone beseeching. "Don't, Graye. Please, let's go home."

"This my woman. Mine. You come in here puttin' yo' hands on my woman and think you gone get away with it. Well, you wrong!"

On the other side of the yard Miss Jen Pearl called out to her son. "Graye, put that gun down! This my birthday. Don't you be startin' no trouble on my birthday!"

Graye, dropping his hand ever so slightly, glanced toward his mother, and the abrasive stare that commanded his obedience. Then from the corner of his eye he caught Tate staring once again toward Angelette, and Jack Daniel's pulled the trigger, sending a round of bullets into Tate Butler's chest.

TWO

Miss Jen Pearl sat with her back against the brick wall, gently stroking the broken girl's brow. Tears had dried against the smooth curvature of the young woman's cheeks and the sobs that had racked her petite frame had eased their way into a deep slumber. Though stiffness was settling into her joints Miss Jen Pearl refused to move. She refused to disturb the moment of peace that had finally settled over Angelette.

As the first sign of a morning sun peeked through the trees she thought about her child and the possessive need he'd had for the young woman against her lap. Graye had been the youngest of her children, the child she'd thought she'd wanted when she'd inhaled and knew she hadn't when she'd exhaled. Her mother had called Graye a change of life baby, coming when no one expected him, least of all Miss Jen Pearl. She'd started birthing children when she'd been sixteen, the eighth one coming just after her twenty-third birthday. Nine years later Graye had pushed his way into the world without asking, without invitation, his presence almost a given like the sun and the moon were givens. Miss Jen Pearl had been thirty-two years old, too old in her mind to be birthing another baby.

She'd had nine children in all. Treat, Sonn, Carr, August and Graye, and the four girls, Lake, Ginn, Sister and July. All of them good and decent, except for Graye, the child tainted with an ugly too difficult to describe. From the moment he'd drawn his first breath evil had wrapped itself around the boy, feeding on his soul.

From inside the house, music whispered past the curtained windows. Jazz was her spirit of choice. The intense vibratos of Coltrane, Ellington, and Fitzgerald were some of her favorites. *Jelly, Jelly* was playing on the new CD player Graye had bought her for her birthday, sending a sultry breeze through the small home. Graye had always been buying something for her, despite her protests for him to save his money so that he and Angelette could buy themselves a house of their own. He had never paid her any never mind though, preferring to be habitually late with the rent on the small cottage his brother owned across the way. Money had seeped from Graye's pockets like water from a cup with no bottom to it. And, no matter how often she had tried to help, to tell him what he needed to do to change, Graye hadn't cared. Miss Jen Pearl heaved a deep sigh.

Miss Jen Pearl couldn't help but think about Tate Butler's mama crying on the other side of town. She could envision the mother's mournful sobs over her dead son's stolen breath, her lament over her baby's soul being dragged to the other side. Hard as she tried though Miss Jen Pearl couldn't find the tears to spill for any of them, least of all her own child, knowing that on the other side of town Mrs. Butler's tears were filling enough buckets for them all.

The morning sun was edging its way precariously through the blue-black sky vibrating in breathtaking hues of pink and orange. Beneath her palm, the young woman's body stiffened ever so slightly then began to shake. Miss Jen Pearl whispered into the morning air. "Shhhhh. It's okay, Baby Doll. It's all gonna be okay." Angelette's quivering frame shook her out of her sleep, and as she opened her eyes, searching anxiously about, Miss Jen Pearl clucked under her breath. "Tch. Tch. I'se right here, Baby Doll. I'se right here. You okay?"

Angelette inhaled deeply then nodded her head. Truth be told she was far from okay and Miss Jen Pearl knew it, but it fit them both to pretend otherwise, if only for a moment.

Thoughts of her husband flashed through her mind. Angelette thought back to the times when they'd laughed until her sides ached, glee spewing from the center of her soul. The memories were bitter-sweet though for just as easily as there could be tears of joy between them, the tears could quickly become ones of pain. The one memory that now pulled hardest was that gun pressed against her heart as Graye pulled the trigger and the loud click of the empty chamber resonating in the dark night while blood dripped like wet paint from the holes in Tate Butler's chest.

Angelette rose to her knees, smoothing damp palms against her crinkled dress. Miss Jen Pearl shifted her stiff limbs. The arthritis in her legs twinged ever so slightly, the invasion of hurt forewarning yet another burden for her to have to suffer with through the day.

"Help me up, Baby Doll. Arthur playin' mean with me this mornin'," she said, extending her arm up toward Angelette.

"I'm sorry Mama Pearl. I didn't mean to have you sittin' out here all night with me."

Miss Jen Pearl smiled a tired smile. "I wasn't, Baby Doll. You was spendin' it with me."

Angelette braced herself to pull Miss Jen Pearl's weight up off the ground and when both women stood firm on their feet, she wrapped her mother-in-law in a deep embrace, her thin arms swallowing the older woman whole. Tears pulled at the edge of Angelette's eyes, but her mother-in-law shook her head, wiping at the woman's face with her fingers.

"Gonna make us some biscuits this morning. Lake made some fresh apple butter yesterday. Apple butter gonna taste nice on some hot biscuits," Miss Jen Pearl said, easing herself through the doorway. ""Yes, yes", she murmured, her voice fading off into the distance. "Gonna taste nice on some hot biscuits."

The McAdams family spilled in and out of Miss Jen Pearl's kitchen, flowing over into the living room and out into the rear yard. Someone had put a CD into the new CD player and soft refrains of jazz played softly in the background. Nana Leah stood in front of the kitchen stove stirring a pot of okra and tomatoes, occasionally leaning down to peek through the oven door at a chicken that was roasting in a large metal pan. Every few minutes her thin voice would break through the noise to bark out a command.

"Jen Pearl, you need to put a pot of rice on. Can't have no okra without no rice."

Miss Jen Pearl nodded. "Mama, please, sit down. I know I got to do the rice, but I can't cook wit' you in my way."

The elder woman bristled at her daughter's frankness, shifting her weight against the metal walker she used. At the table, Ginn and Sister laughed loudly as the two women bickered back and forth between themselves until Nana Leah finally gave in and took a seat. In the center of the table a mound of shucked corn waited patiently for the pot of boiling water that sat on the back burner.

The back door opened and then closed behind Angelette who carried a tray of barbecued ribs that Sonn had just taken off the grill. The bantering between him and his brothers wafted in with the smoky aroma of the succulent meat.

"Sonn said this meat is done and it won't be much longer for the rest of it."

"Be sure it's done," Nana Leah responded. "You got to be sure with pork. You got to cook pork good." Her head bobbed up and down against her fragile neck.

Miss Jen Pearl rolled her eyes, taking the tray out of Angelette's hands. "I'll check it, Mama," she said, shouting loudly enough for the woman to hear.

Nana Leah nodded her head, rocking her body in the chair. "You got to cook pork good." Nana Leah gestured toward Angelette, extending her good hand, the one that had not been affected by the stroke. At the age of ninety-three, Nana Leah's body had long begun to fail her, but her mind was still as crisp and sharp as the day she was born. "Come sit down, Baby Doll," she said, patting the chair beside her. "Have yo'self a seat."

Angelette dropped into the thinly padded chair, smiling a faint smile at her husband's sisters as she did.

Ginn leaned over to squeeze her shoulder. "How you doin', Angelette?"

The woman nodded her head slowly. "I'm okay."

Sister glanced quickly toward her mother and back to Angelette. "Well, you're better than I would be. If my husband had tried to kill me you all would be visiting me in my bed."

Miss Jen Pearl sucked her teeth as the rice and salted water started to simmer. She turned the gas flame down to low and turned toward the conversation. "Sister you stay in yo' bed. It don't take much to get you to fall into it."

The girls laughed. July entered the room with her newborn infant on her shoulder. She leaned to hug Angelette, who reached out to take the baby from her arms. "July, he is so sweet," Angelette gushed, pressing her nose into the powder-scented folds around the child's chubby neck.

"I don't know about sweet", she answered, dropping a cloth diaper onto Angelette's shoulder. "He don't do nothin' but cry."

Miss Jen Pearl laughed. "Change a life babies is like that. They know you too tired and they work hard to wear you down. And wit' them two roughnecks for brothers I'd cry too if I was him. Those twins of yours been worryin' this child crazy since he come home from the hospital. Every time I look they want to be holdin' 'em or kissin' on 'em. Baby can't get no good rest."

July laughed, striding to the other side of the table to take a seat. "Them boys in there right now huggin' on Amber," she said of her seven-year-old twins, Collin and Dillon.

Ginn raised her eyebrows. "Don't you let them boys hurt my baby."

"Yo' baby ain't no baby anymore. That girl is twelve-years old acting like she grown and when she get tired of them boys she'll make 'em stop. I saw how she pinched Dillon last week. Left a bruise the size of a lemon on his arm."

Ginn sucked her teeth, rolling her eyes at her sister.

July continued. "Besides, yo' brother's wife has got her eyes on all of 'em."

Nana Leah squinted her eyes. "What brother's wife? Who wife in there?"

Miss Jen Pearl shook her head. "Carr's wife, Mama. Irene."

"When Carr get himself a wife?"

"Carr done had him two wives, Mama. Where you been?"

Angelette giggled, shifting the baby against her shoulder.

"I can't keep up wit' all yo' children. They got more wives and babies than the good Lord should allow."

"I know that's right", Sister interjected. "Don't you worry, Nana Leah. I can barely keep up myself."

Laughter rang through the room, then died out quietly as everyone fell into their own thoughts. From the front room children's laughter danced off the walls. Miss Jen Pearl looked from one face to the next, resting her gaze on Angelette and the longing in the woman's eyes as she cuddled the infant against her chest.

Miss Jen Pearl could read her thoughts as clearly as if they were printed in dark ink on ivory paper. Angelette and Graye had been together for almost ten years and Angelette had not been able to have any children. Last year when it had become an issue between them Graye had gone out and gotten Maxine Wallace pregnant. Angelette had hung her head in shame, heart-broken over the betrayal, and through it all, she'd still gone on loving Graye.

Maxine's baby had died shortly after it was born. Nana Leah had said it was a silent blessing, the angels taking the small bundle home to heaven. She'd declared it God's way of correcting Graye's mistake. After that, Graye and Angelette had gone on like nothing had happened. But Miss Jen Pearl knew that a piece of Angelette had died that day too. Her son's ambivalent attitude toward the loss of his only child had been illuminating. Graye had no more wanted to be a father than the man in the moon, but he'd wanted to prove that it was Angelette's fault that they had no children. Once he'd planted his seed and saw it to fruition, he too had been thankful that he had no other responsibilities than that initial watering had demanded of him. The women at the table all heaved a heavy sigh simultaneously, blowing hot breath across the room, and Angelette pulled July's baby just a little closer to her heart.

"You gone burn that rice," Nana Leah interjected, breaking the silence.

"The rice is fine, Mama," Miss Jen Pearl responded, rising to lift the metal top from the pan. The faint mist of steam rising off the white of the rice brushed warm against her face. As she pulled the prongs of a long fork through the cooked grain to insure all the water had boiled away, Miss Jen Pearl suddenly wanted to fling the iron pot and its contents across the room. She could feel the tears rising as she struggled to contain the anger that suddenly consumed her.

Where had she failed she thought to herself as she quickly glanced from the face of one daughter to the other. Where had she failed her youngest son? It was her own mother's eyes, that all-knowing stare that stilled the swell within her heart. Nana Leah reached out a fragile hand toward her only child, caressing the length of the woman's arm. She nodded her gray head, clucking lightly under her breath.

"Don't you go burnin' 'dis rice now," she said quietly. "We can't be havin' no burnt rice."

Miss Jen Pearl could feel the intensity passing as her mother rose to press wrinkled lips against her skin, brushing the sepia of her own cheek against Miss Jen Pearl's.

Side by side one could not help but notice the striking resemblance between them. The duo had aged beautifully, the clarity of their complexions belying their respective ages. Of average height, their bodies were fuller now, breasts rounder, hips wider, waists thicker. It was obvious that they had both been exquisite during their younger years for they were both extremely beautiful. But one had only to look at the generation of women around the table to see just how still the waters of beauty ran through the family line.

What usually first caught the attention of strangers was the magnificence of their mouths, full, pouty lips which beckoned to be kissed. What held their attention was the dark vibrancy of their large, black eyes, the thick length of their blue-black hair and the rich caramel coloration of their crystal clear complexions. The two older women were both totally gray now, the color of their hair as white as newly fallen snow. And though the younger women still allowed theirs to fall pass their shoulders, no one ever saw Nana Leah's hair or Miss Jen Pearl's out of the French braids, intricate twists and buns they wore daily.

The women around the table fell silent as they pretended not to notice the interaction between the matriarchs of their family. They pretended not to see Miss Jen Pearl's distress, the agony across her face that had caused Nana Leah to rise from her seat and wrap her good arm around Miss Jen Pearl's shoulders. Later, they all ignored the faint burnt of brown that coated the rice upon their plates.

THREE

Hers had been a warm kind of loving when he had let it be, her long limbs wrapped around him like a much needed blanket on a crisp January morning. The heat that rose from her skin had spun a vibrant warmth up and over him, and as he'd rested his head along the round of her breasts, he'd wanted only to snuggle deep beneath the essence of her, and melt the chill from his soul.

His need for her had become unnatural, his craving stirred by the mere thought of her flesh against his flesh. Just the whisper of her name would waken his manhood and command him to possess her. October, just before the birth of his son, had been the last time he could remember her giving herself willingly, wanting to feel his touch against her skin. Then she'd gone cold with the chill of the season and his desire had become an obsession. Refusing to accept what he saw in her eyes, he abused the love between her legs, taking what he believed to be his as she lay in apathy beneath him.

Ignoring the torment she'd been made to endure at his hands, he'd blamed others for her transformation. He'd blamed the women who'd told her she could do better, and the men who stood waiting for his back to be turned. And he blamed Tate who'd not bothered to hide his longing, always caressing her fears with a gentle smile. He'd seen Tate hug her once, wrapping himself around her hurt. And, as intensely as his friend had wished away the woman's pain, had Graye wished away his friend.

His hand dropped to his crotch, gently cupping the limp flesh. The metal bars beneath the thin mattress pressed angry against his back. Tears dripped quietly from Graye's eyes. His worst nightmares had come true and it was all over now. His best friend was dead and he imagined he would never again feel the warmth of his woman's loving.

Miss Jen Pearl cursed God today. The conservative Baptist congregation she worshiped with weekly would have been thoroughly appalled at the profanity she slung in the good Lord's direction. She'd had a bone to pick with the Almighty though and candy-coating her displeasure would not have served either of them well. She'd ask for forgiveness later she thought, holding tight to the bible that said she needed only to ask for absolution for it to be given. The Baptist congregation would not have been quite so accommodating.

She sat alone in the narrow hallway of the Orange County Courthouse, watching as a burly, red-faced officer checked the short length of chain around her son's hands and feet before escorting the man out of the building and into a waiting prison bus. She sat alone because she'd forbidden her other children to come with her. Graye had forbidden Angelette. As Graye had passed his mother he'd refused to lift his eyes to acknowledge her, feigning disinterest at her presence. He'd forbidden her to attend also and she had found it necessary to remind him just who was the parent and who was the child.

When Miss Jen Pearl had been able to look Graye in the eye and spew the words that told him what she thought of him, it had been a point of revelation for her. In that brief moment, as he'd endured the verbal blows she threw and she'd witnessed the tears that had clouded his vision, she truly understood the propensity within her that enabled her to cause another human-being pain. For this, she cursed God, for never in her wildest dreams could she have ever imagined bringing her baby boy such hurt.

The state of North Carolina had indicted Graye on a charge of second degree murder. In response, Drake Tyler, Graye's friend, the attorney, had entered a plea of not guilty on her son's behalf. Ms. Jen Pearl could only shake her head at that. Her child had stood before the judge, a young man who barely looked thirty and had lied, nodding his head in agreement that he was not guilty of the crime fifty-two people saw him commit. Bail had been denied.

Graye's attorney tilted his head toward her, gesturing for her attention. Miss Jen Pearl waited him out, barely raising an eyebrow to look in the man's direction. If he wanted to speak with her he would have to come to where she was she thought not bothering to rise from where she sat. She had no intentions of jumping simply because he said so. The man was a fool. Lying that Graye was not guilty. The man was a bigger fool than Graye was. A look of total disgust graced her face as he finally made his way over to her side, taking a seat beside her.

"Good morning, Miss McAdams," he said, swiping at the sweat across his brow with a dingy white handkerchief. "I hope you're well this morning?"

"Well as can be expected, Mr. Tyler."

The man nodded, inhaling deeply. "We've got a long fight ahead of us, Miss McAdams. I'm going to need all the help I can get to free Graye."

"Why? Graye did it. Everybody saw it. What's there to fight about?"

The man cleared his throat. "There were extenuating circumstances, of course. This being a crime of passion we can show that your son was not thinking rationally. That he acted in a moment of emotional distress that caused him to lose control of his mental faculties. We're going to prove he acted during a moment of insanity."

Miss Jen Pearl studied the man closely. Sweat beaded in small pools across his brow, along the length of his nose, toward the crest of his chin. His skin was pale and pasty, his flesh like wet dough. An immaculately tailored navy blue suit fit his thick frame nicely though, the long line of the expensive fabric falling gracefully across his wide shoulders. He continued to swipe at the moisture along his face and although the air was still in the room Miss Jen Pearl knew it was not the heat that caused him to sweat so profusely. Men who lied tended to sweat more than men who didn't.

Rising to her feet she brushed her hands down the length of her cotton shift then adjusted her large white purse on her shoulder. Mr. Tyler rose with her, still waiting for a response. Miss Jen Pearl looked him up and down before opening her mouth, her gaze racing from the top of his dirty-blond hair to the tip of his black patent leather shoes and back again.

"Graye killed that man. Won't nothin' insane about him when he did it. It was evil, pure and simple. If he gets away with it you can bet there will be one more dead body for you to say he didn't kill before all is done and finished. You can bet on that."

Dismissing the man with a quick shake of her head, she spun around on her heels and exited the building. Outside, the bright sunlight rained over her as she made her way down the concrete steps. Graye watched his mother from behind the bus windows, her aged body framed by the metal bars outside the glass. There was nothing more that needed to be said

Miss Jen Pearl thought to herself, her eyes locked firmly on Graye's. Although his gaze was brief it took her breath away and she inhaled deeply fighting to fill her lungs with oxygen. If looks could kill she thought she knew she'd surely be standing dead.

Relief flooded her spirit when Graye closed his eyes and shook the fury from his brow. When he reopened them, connecting his gaze with hers for a second time, the look was different, no longer bitter, no longer angry. This time his spirit was calm, the fury no longer washing over his soul and he smiled, blowing his mother a kiss. As the bus driver shifted the large vehicle out of park and eased it into traffic, mother and son continued to stare each other down and it was only when her son's eyes were out of her sight that Miss Jen Pearl headed for home.

FOUR

Graye bristled as the guard closed the heavy iron door behind him. The man on the other side of the bars grinned widely as Graye heaved a deep sigh.

"Told you we'd see each other again didn't I, McAdams," the man stated smugly. "Told you from the get go that you ain't had it in you to do right on the outside. Seems like you gone be with us for a long time this go round. You done messed up good this time."

Graye smiled slightly, dropping onto the lower bunk of his cell. "I just missed your pretty face, Officer Burke. Had to come back to see it one more time."

Burke laughed. "Told you if you keep pissing on people one day you was gone get pissed back on. Now look at you. What you kill that boy for anyway? Won't he your friend?"

Graye's smile faded. "He won't no boy. Tate was a grown man. You show him some respect."

"Well, he dead now and he got you to thank for it. Where was your respect? Some friend you turned out to be."

Graye's faded smile shifted into a scowl as he glared through the bars. Burke flinched as Graye's eyes narrowed and the line of his jaw tightened. The muscles in Graye's arms tensed as he balled his right fist into the palm of his left hand. Instinctively the guard's hand dropped to the head of the nightstick at his waist. He stepped back ever so slightly. Graye could suddenly smell the man's fear, a pervasive stench that filled the distance between them. He laughed as he leaned back to stretch the length of his body across the thin mattress. With a wave of his hand Graye brushed at the air in Burke's direction, brushing the man away like one might flick away a fly. Graye's laughter continued to fill the air, joining the evening noise that filled the confines of the cell block. Graye's laughter followed Burke past the row of locked cages and continued as the heavy doors at the end of the corridor were closed behind him.

"Lights out!" The verbal warning barely preceded the outpour of darkness that suddenly filled the small space.

Graye shifted his body onto his side, preferring to face the cement blocks instead of the barred wall. He inhaled deeply, blowing hot breath onto the thin pillow beneath his head. Reaching to scratch at his bald head Graye's thoughts eased back to another time and another place when all had been well with him and Tate.

The boys had both been twelve years old when Tate Butler's family had moved from New York City to Anson County. It had been July 1979 and the summer heat had a firm hold on the fertile land that swept from one county line to the other. The air was humid and moisture filled Tate Butler's lungs as he ran from his house across the railroad tracks to the woods down by the Tucker farmstead. It was a faint cry that caught his attention, a minute wail that begged for attention. His search for the source of the cry led him deep into the woods and when he was just on the verge of being afraid that he was lost, he stumbled upon the likes of Graye McAdams and a small black puppy Graye had by the throat. They locked eyes as Graye's other hand held a large rock over the animal's head. Stepping in closer Tate continued to stare Graye down.

"You gone kill that dog?"

"What's it to you?"

Tate shrugged. "It ain't nothin' to me. I was just askin'."

Graye's hold on the rock tightened. "You want to see me smash its brains in?"

Tate shrugged, his gaze still locked on Graye's face. "What's yo' name?"

The other boy narrowed his eyes, digging his fingers tighter into the pup's neck. The creature yelped ever so slightly, crying out for release.

Tate continued to talk, not bothering to wait for a response. "My name's Tate. Tate Butler. I just come from New York."

Graye's eyes widened. "You from the city?"

Tate nodded his head. "Was born in Harlem. Been there all my life until now. You from here?"

Graye nodded.

Tate walked to Graye's side, leaning to peer down at the dog. "You do any huntin' for big animals like deer and stuff or you just like pickin' on puppies?"

Graye smiled. "I hunt. This my sister's dog and she took my dollar that I got for cartin' lumber for ol' man Simms. I tol' her if she didn't give me my dollar back I was gone get even wit' her."

Tate nodded his head again, then reached into his back pocket pulling his money into his hands. "I'll give you two dollars if you give me that dog. My mama likes dogs and it's gone be her birthday soon. I can give her that puppy as a present."

Graye stared at the money that filled Tate's palms and without a second thought dropped the rock to the ground. As he reached for the money with one hand, he shoved the puppy toward Tate with his other. "You stupid for giving away yo' money fo' some dumb dog."

Tate shrugged as he pulled the frightened animal close to his chest. "Maybe. But you ain't too bright for wantin' to break its head with a rock either. A dead dog won't gone make yo' sister give you yo dollar back."

Graye laughed, smoothing the two bills between the round of his fingers. "My name's Graye. My friends call me Graye."

Tate smiled. "You got friends?"

Graye laughed again. "I do now."

Graye led the way out of the woods as Tate continued to hold tight to the dog, stroking the warmth of its fur. As the small animal settled against his chest, sensing the hold around it had gone from deadly to protective, it quieted down and fell into a restful sleep. Back across the train tracks and onto the main roadway, Graye continued to lead the way until they found themselves in front of the McAdams' home. Graye's mother stood on the front porch watching as they made their way down the street, into the yard and up the front steps. Her gaze stopped them in their tracks.

"Where you been, Graye?"

The boy shrugged his shoulders, stubbing the toe of his worn sneakers into the dirt below. Miss Jen Pearl shook her head, sucking her teeth.

"Won't you supposed to go wit' yo' daddy to help over at the Mason's farm?

Graye shrugged again, still not bothering to respond. Anger blessed his mother's face, the rising ire swelling in the dark of her large eyes. Her gaze moved from Graye to Tate and the small puppy that lay in the young man's arms.

"Who are you?"

"Tate Butler, ma'am. I'm a friend a Graye's."

Graye cut his eyes in the other boy's direction and nodded ever so slightly.

Miss Jen Pearl shook her head, waving it up and down on her shoulders. "Why you got Sister's dog?"

"It's my dog, ma'am. I paid two dollars for 'em."

Graye glanced from Tate to his mother and back toward the dirt that he'd pushed into a small pile before him.

"You pay Graye for that dog?"

"Yes, ma'am. Two dollars."

"Graye, how you go sellin' yo' sister's dog? That won't yo' dog to be givin' away."

Graye spoke up for the first time. "Sister took my dollar that I got fo' workin' fo' Mr. Simms. I had to get my dollar back."

His mother shook her head. "How you know Sister took yo' dollar?"

"Cause I had it and she was the only one who knowed where I put it and it went gone."

"So you took her dog and sold it."

Graye looked up defiantly. "I was gone kill it but then this fool come long and want to buy it from me."

His mother gasped slightly at her son's frankness, her eyes searching the lines of his young face for some sign of remorse. "Why was you gone kill Sister's dog?"

The boy's eyes dropped back down to the ground. "She took my dollar," he muttered under his breath.

Miss Jen Pearl reached into the pocket of her house dress and pulled a wrinkled dollar bill from the folds. "I found this dollar in yo' pants pocket when I went to do the wash. Is this the dollar you said Sister stole?"

Graye looked up in surprise. Miss Jen Pearl nodded her head. "That's right. It was in yo' pocket and here you were about to kill a little dog over it, wantin' to blame Sister."

Graye reached out for the money in his mother's hand. Miss Jen Pearl pulled it back out of his reach and put it back into her pocket. "Let me see the two dollars you got now."

Her son hesitated, shifting his weight from one foot to the other before doing as he was told. Miss Jen Pearl took one of the dollar bills from him, folded it and added it to the bill in the pocket of her house coat.

"This money belongs to Sister. That's what you got for her dog."

Graye bristled. "She can have her old dog back." He looked over at Tate, his eyes stating his intent.

Miss Jen Pearl shook her head. "Well then yo' friend will get his money back but you don't get it. You got yo' dollar."

"Tch." Graye sucked his teeth, stubbing his toe harder into the dirt.

"If it's alright ma'am I'd like to keep the dog, " Tate interjected, stealing a glance toward Graye.

Miss Jen Pearl studied the boy momentarily, then called for her daughter. "Sister! Sister, come out here!"

Sister McAdams came obediently, wiping her hands against a faded blue and white striped dish towel. At twenty-four she was a replica of her mother, the lines of her delicate face identical to the older woman's standing beside her. A large afro sat atop her head like an over-sized woolen cap, the deep black coloration framing the warm brown of her complexion nicely. A cotton halter-top barely covered her full bustline, accentuating her paper-thin waist and the long length of leg that extended past her cut-off shorts. Tate smiled at her shyly, his eyes dropping to study the top of the puppy's head. Every few seconds he would gaze up at Sister, fighting not to stare so brazenly. The young woman smiled back then turned to glare at her brother.

"Sister, Graye went and sold yo' dog to this boy. His name's Tate Butler. He got two dollars for it. If you want the dog then I'm gone give him his money back. But Tate say he'd like to keep the dog. What would you like?"

Sister studied Graye, then Tate, before responding.

"You stopped my brother from killing that dog didn't you?" she asked softly, her eyes smiling in Tate's direction.

Tate shrugged. "I just paid two dollars fo' it."

She turned to glare at Graye again, shaking her head from side to side. Reaching for the money in her mother's palm, she shook her head. "Keep him. His name's Biscuit. I can get me another one from Miss Simms. She still got two puppies left and she giving 'em away for free," she said as she headed back into the house. "Besides, ain't nothing safe around that evil Graye."

Miss Jen Pearl winced at her daughter's parting words. "Tate, you go on home now. Graye's got work to do."

"Yes, ma'am."

Tate met Graye's eyes only briefly before turning to leave. Hesitating momentarily, he turned back to the porch and the woman who stood waiting for her son to enter the house.

"Ma'am?"

Miss Jen Pearl turned back around to see what the child wanted, her eyebrows raised with curiosity.

"Would it be okay for Graye to come to my house for supper tomorrow night? I want him to meet my folks and if my mama says it's okay, he can even spend the night. If it's okay with you?"

Graye looked at Tate with surprise, his mouth dropping open widely. Miss Jen Pearl nodded her head and smiled. "Come on by tomorrow and if it's okay wit' yo' mama then I guess it'll be okay wit' me. Thank you. Graye's lucky to have such a good friend."

Tate smiled at Graye. "I'm lucky too, ma'am. See you tomorrow, Graye," he called over his shoulder as he made his way out of the yard.

"Yeah," Graye responded, not quite sure how to respond. "Tomorrow."

Side by side, Graye and Miss Jen Pearl watched Tate make his way down the street, that puppy still cradled deep within his arms. When the boy's slight frame was no longer visible Miss Jen Pearl turned to look into her son's face and for the first time, in a long time, she saw Graye smile.

Prison noises pulled Graye from the depths of memory that had dropped him into a light sleep. Sepia-toned reflections of things long since past no longer danced through his mind. Dank shadows of steel bars, burly prison guards, and the stark emptiness of his surroundings spinning him to another channel. He heaved a deep sigh, turning to lie on his back, one arm curled over his head. His body ached, craving something sweeter to nourish the loneliness that surrounded him. In the dead space that billowed over his spirit, he could hear the hushed whisper of voices, distant and foreign against his ears. Somewhere along the corridor a man was crying, his sobs breaking the stillness of quiet between him and Graye. A door slammed, footsteps stomped heavy against the concrete floors, and prison noises continued to pull at Graye until the depths of sleep finally took control.

FIVE

Angelette leaned against the handle of the WalMart shopping cart, waiting patiently as Miss Jen Pearl plucked an arrangement of plastic flowers from a wire display stand. The older woman pushed and pulled at an assortment of color combinations before she was satisfied.

"This should do it," she finally professed, dropping the length of stems into the basket. "This will grow my garden nicely."

Angelette smiled a slow smile that brightened the dull shadows that clouded her face. She'd not smiled since Tate had been killed and they'd taken Graye to the county jail. But the smile quickly faded as thoughts of Tate crossed her mind. She sighed a deep, woeful sigh that caused Miss Jen Pearl to raise an anxious eyebrow.

"Is you okay?"

Angelette nodded, pulling her fingers through the length of her chestnut hair. She could only nod, suddenly fearful that if she spoke she might somehow betray the emotions rising within her.

Miss Jen Pearl read the creased lines that crossed the younger woman's face. There was a story behind the girl's eyes and Miss Jen Pearl instinctively knew it was one she preferred not be told. Stories like that usually caused more harm than good and there had already been enough damage done to them all.

The two women locked eyes and Miss Jen Pearl shook her head ever so slightly. Angelette sighed again, turning away from her mother-in-law's gaze. Miss Jen Pearl's thick voice reached out to shake her. "You needs to plant you a garden. Give yo'self somethin' else to be thinkin' about. Here."

Angelette looked back over her shoulder toward the older woman. Thick bouquets of roses were clenched tightly in Miss Jen Pearl's hand, her short stubby fingers clutched protectively around the artificial stems.

"I'll get you started," she concluded, dropping the arrangement into the basket along side her own selections.

"Where should I plant them?" Angelette asked.

Miss Jen Pearl smiled. "Plant them in the front by the edge of the porch. 'Dat porch could use some color and this red's a real nice color," she said, turning toward another aisle and the other side of the store. Angelette nodded her head slowly as she turned the shopping cart around to catch up with woman.

Miss Jen Pearl had been planting plastic flowers around her yard for as long as anyone could remember. Every year she would change the artificial hues to suit her many moods. Since autumn had set in her colors of choice were bright oranges and shimmery yellows to replace the rich blues, reds and pinks that had lined the flowerbeds during the heat of the summer. Now she wanted Angelette to plant red roses in her own yard. The younger woman smiled to herself, bemused by the absurdity, entertained by the prospect of planting her own plastic garden in her yard.

Miss Jen Pearl continued to drop items into the basket, adding a twelve-roll pack of toilet tissue, a box of size nine envelopes, two bottles of lemon scented amnonia, and a pack of Juicy-Fruit chewing gum. Standing in the checkout line, Angelette watched as Miss Jen Pearl pulled a roll of bills wrapped tightly within a rubber band from her cleavage. Miss Jen Pearl, like her mother, carried her possessions close to her heart, locked between the expanse of mammary tissue and the fabric of her brassiere. Angelette could not help but smile again as the woman pushed her funds back between her breasts.

Miss Jen Pearl returned the smile, grinning broadly. "That's better," she said, removing the neatly bagged purchases from the countertop. "You are much too pretty to be wearin' such a long face all the time."

Angelette blushed as she shook her head in disagreement.

"Now what I say," Miss Jen Pearl responded. "All of my girls is beautiful." She reached out to stroke the length of Angelette's face with her free hand.

"We can't go back and change things, Baby Doll. So the best thing for us to do is keep on going and keep trying to do better."

Tears rose to Angelette's eyes, threatening to spill past her long lashes.

"Now, now, none of that," Miss Jen Pearl said, clucking her teeth as she pushed Angelette out of the door. "We has to go plant us some flowers."

SIX

Want of a man can be an all-consuming want, the need of him spreading like cancerous cells over vital flesh. It can steal a woman's sanity like a masked bandit on a dark mission, rendering her useless. With control lost, it's as if her person has been snapped like a twig under the step of a heavy foot. For a woman like Angelette, the want of a man had taken her soul on a journey that was going to be difficult for her to come back from.

Staring out over the front steps to the bright red roses she could feel a storm brewing, a series of warm fronts just waiting to collide. It hung heavy in the humid air, much like the heavy that hung over her heart. She inhaled deeply, fighting to fill her lungs with the rancid air that burned hot with moisture. But the humidity made it difficult to breathe and so Angelette looked forward to the storm that promised to bring thunderous relief. Angelette yearned for relief, a soothing mist of cool that could ease the rising tension within her.

In the distance one could hear the roar of thunder rolling across the sky in her direction and off in the horizon she caught her first glimpse of lightning. As dark murky clouds painted the sky a hazy gray, Angelette sat mesmerized by the burst of color that snapped like photographic images across her mind. Memories of Graye spilled over her thoughts and she remembered back to a time when it had just been her and him and all had been well between them.

Something else had been on his mind as he sat rocking back and forth against a wooden chair. He had definitely not been thinking of her when she'd sauntered naked to his side and had straddled her body around him and that chair. Nuzzling her face into his neck she'd kissed the spot just behind his ear, running her tongue slowly around the curve of his earlobe. Graye had tasted sweet, and she had muttered her appreciation against his skin. As she pressed the lip of her pelvic bone against the zipper of his cream-colored painter's pants, she settled her mouth against his. She kissed him hungrily, feasting on his lips as he kissed her just as deeply. His tongue danced inside her mouth, and she welcomed him, savoring every ounce of the moment.

Reaching her hands beneath his bleached-white, tank top, she'd caressed the faint line of baby fine hair that ran along the length of his chest. Lust burned hot from her fingertips, scorching his flesh. The warmth of his breath tickled the flesh along her neck as he blew a heavy sigh against her skin, his mouth dropping to her shoulder to skate down the length of her arm. Heat raged through his groin, the length of his dick rising to attention. Graye whimpered ever so slightly, wrapping one arm tightly around her waist as the other reached for a protruding nipple that pressed hard against the flat of his palm.

Motioning as though to rise from where he sat had made her tighten her legs around him. "Don't," she'd whispered softly, "I want on top, like this, right here."

Graye had chuckled, reaching between them to ease his zipper open and release himself from his pants. The protuberant tissue snaked eagerly between her thighs, suddenly lost in the heat of her sanctuary. Graye's chuckle faded to a low groan as Angelette began to ride his manhood, the whole of himself filling her.

They'd rocked against the back of the padded chair, their rhythmic gyrations smooth and controlled. Graye had marveled at how neatly they fit together, the line of his flesh matching each crease and fold of her. Her muscles had tightened around him, squeezing and pulling at him, forcing all of him deep within her until he was fighting to hold on. Her body had burned hot against his and Graye had gasped for air, feeling as though he might suffocate beneath the intensity of the heat. Angelette had brushed her full breasts against his chest, their nipples locked in a delicate kiss between them, and when she'd screamed, crying out his name in pleasure, it was as if her whole body had become his, all of Graye exploding through her bloodstream.

A raging crack of thunder slapped the memory from Angelette's mind as the sky opened up over head and the rain spilled down around her. Wiping the trickle of moisture from her eyes Angelette eased her way inside the house and behind her the rain washed down over her plastic roses.

From where she stood in her living room window Miss Jen Pearl quietly watched Angelette rocking her lean frame on the steps of her small home. She was still watching when the sky spilled water down over the girl, running her inside. The old woman blew a deep sigh as the elderly man behind her coughed lightly for her attention.

"Are you alright, Jen Pearl?" he asked, shifting ever so slightly in the chair beneath him. "Can I get you anything?" Concern spilled out of his blue eyes, flooding the room with tense emotion.

Miss Jen Pearl turned her attention back to her guest, smiling a faint smile in the man's direction. Dr. Horace Burton smiled back, the gesture barely lifting the deep creases of his aged face.

'I'm sorry, Doc Burton. I'm just fine. I was just looking at that sky out there. Looks like it's gone be a quick shower this afternoon. Sun's sittin' off to the east just waitin' to come back out," she professed. Dr. Burton nodded.

"Can I get you another piece of pie?" Miss Jen Pearl asked politely, reaching for the empty porcelain plate that rested lightly on his knee.

"No, ma'am. That sure was some good pie though. I only get good pie like that when I come here."

"Well you know you're welcome for pie here any time," she laughed, setting the empty plate onto the low coffee table.

Dr. Burton nodded again, the silver stands of his thinning hair flapping atop his head. Silence enveloped the room once again as Miss Jen Pearl settled herself comfortably on the sofa directly across from the recliner that Dr. Burton sat in. She watched him closely as he twisted his fingers in a knot, the aged appendages gnarled like ancient tree roots.

"You looks like a man that wants to say somethin', Doc," she said, breaking the silence between them. "What be on your mind this afternoon?"

Dr. Burton cleared his throat, paused, then cleared it a second time before speaking. "I just wanted you to know that if you need anything that I'm here. I know it ain't been easy for you with all that's been going on with your boy. If I can be of any help..." The words caught in the old man's throat as his eyes attempted to finish the sentence for him. His gaze met hers only briefly before searching the patterned rug on the floor at his feet. He suddenly felt like a school boy. The embarrassment was getting the better of him.

Miss Jen Pearl smiled and nodded, reaching up to brush a wisp of hair from her brow. Although the duo had known each other since forever there was still a thin edge of formality that wafted between them and Miss Jen Pearl suddenly laughed out loud bemused by the hilarity of the tension they shared.

"Doc Burton, I do declare," she exclaimed, her gaze darting around the room to avoid the man's eyes.

Dr. Burton blushed profusely, a bright tinge of crimson painting the alabaster of his cheeks. "I...I..." He stammered for words.

The moment was interrupted as Miss Jen Pearl's daughters rushed into the room. Miss Jen Pearl narrowed her eyes as she appraised Ginn and Sister and the noise that came flooding inside with them. Long and lanky like their father had been, her girls were paper thin tornadoes of loud noise. Even when they were just knee high Miss Jen Pearl had marveled at how you could always hear them even before you could see them.

"Hey, Mama," the two women called out in unison. "Good afternoon, Dr. Burton."

Dr. Burton rose to his feet, extending his hand first toward Ginn and then Sister. "How are you girls doing?" he asked politely.

"We're just fine, sir," Ginn answered as she leaned down to hug her mother, the length of her freshly braided extensions brushing down over her mother's shoulders. Miss Jen Pearl grabbed a handful of synthetic tresses, the expression on her face voicing her dislike of her child's newest hairdo.

"Did I invite you two over here today?" Miss Jen Pearl asked, raising the same thick eyebrows each of her daughters possessed.

Sister chuckled lightly. "No, ma'am, but we were at the beauty parlor and Miss Harris sent you some dinner." Sister gestured toward the picnic basket in her hands. "She made us promise to bring it right over."

Miss Jen Pearl pursed her lips, the lines around her mouth tightening. "She did, did she?"

"Miss Harris was just being nice, Mama, " Ginn said, instantly reading her mother's reaction.

"She just trying to get in my business is what she doing. Andra-Bell know she can't cook a lick, talking 'bout she sending someone dinner."

Sister lifted the lid of the basket. "It looks good to me. Baked ham, macaroni and cheese, corn bread..."

Miss Jen Pearl frowned at her daughter, flipping her hand in the air. "Take that mess into the kitchen, please." She lifted the empty pie plate from the table and extended it toward Sister. "Take this with you and wash up them dirty dishes in the sink."

The two women exchanged a look between them before making an obedient exit.

Dr. Burton chuckled as he crossed the room to take a seat beside Miss Jen Pearl. "You are too hard on folks, Jen Pearl," he said lightly, reaching to take her hand in his.

Miss Jen Pearl eyed him out of the corner of her eye, sucking her teeth. Dr. Burton continued. "Folks care. They just want to show you how much you and your family mean to them. You and your mama been taking care of everybody else for so long and now people just want to take care of you." He lifted her hand to his lips and kissed the back of her fingers ever so slightly. The warmth of his breath washed over her hand, and up the length of her arm. "I want to take care of you, Jen Pearl, if you'd let me," he finished.

Miss Jen Pearl cut her eyes at Dr. Burton, her lips lifted in a faint smile. As he held onto her hand she studied his pale appendages just as she'd studied them the first time they'd met. It had been almost fifty years ago right after she'd given birth to July. She had just celebrated her twenty-third birthday. A nasty pelvic infection had stifled her usual vibrancy and Dr. Horace Burton, one of only two doctors in town, had been the only one willing to make a house call to a colored family on the west side of town. He'd been making regular house calls to check on her and her children ever since.

Back then neither would have ever publically acknowledged any attraction for the other. The tide of that time would have made any union between them duplicitous, both knowing the unspoken laws where a white man and black woman did not mix out in the open where they might be seen. Both of their forefathers would have been spinning somersaults in their respective graves if anyone had even dared to imagine that they might actually respect, love, and want to be together.

So Dr. Burton had his wife and Miss Jen Pearl stayed married to Odell McAdams. Some twenty years ago, both of their spouses had died within two years of each other. Odell had passed first, the victim of an automobile accident and Dr. Burton's wife, Livia, died from cancer after an extended illness. The two had sought comfort in each other's company and the friendship between them had thrived. They'd grown old together, keeping their friendship at arms length despite an aching desire that may have seeped past their eyes when one or the other let their guard down.

The doctor's hands were older now. Age spotted the pale flesh, the loose skin clinging for dear life to fragile bones. His hands though tired, were still strong and Miss Jen Pearl marveled at the skill within those fingers that had healed and helped many a patient over the years. Once, many many moons ago, Miss Jen Pearl had imagined those hands against the brown of her skin, brushing ever so lightly down the length of her body. She'd marveled at the thought of his whiteness against her own rich chocolate complexion. The possibility of their hues blending into the faintest of browns had excited her. She blushed at the memory. Too much time had passed for either of them to be giving any notion to such nonsense Miss Jen Pearl thought. She pulled her hand from his, clasping it close to her chest. The memories had left her flustered. His touch had taken her breath.

"You wants somethin' to eat," she asked, changing the subject. "Maybe some of Andra-Bell Harris' dinner?"

Dr. Burton sighed, shaking his head no. "I declare woman. You do know how to try a man's patience."

"You an old fool, Doc. Both of us too old to be thinking 'bout such nonsense. I ain't studying you."

Dr. Burton laughed, leaning over to kiss Miss Jen Pearl's cheek. "Both of us might be old, but that doesn't mean..."

Miss Jen Pearl interrupted him. "You are my best friend, Horace. You and me will always be friends. We know what we feel. We don't need to talk about it. Just leave things be. Right now I've got to worry about Graye and Angelette and the rest of Otis McAdams' children."

"You've been worryin' 'bout Otis McAdams' children since I met you."

"And I'm gone worry 'bout 'em until the day I die."

Dr. Burton smiled again, waving his head from side to side.

Miss Jen Pearl rose from where she sat to go look out the window one more time. Dr. Burton rose with her, standing beside her as she pulled back the sheer white curtain to peer outside. The rain had passed just as quickly as she'd predicted and the sun loomed brightly in the sky. Both noted the bright red flowers across the road, lining the length of the front porch of the house before them.

Miss Jen Pearl sighed deeply. "When my boy was born it was stormin' just like it did earlier. Except there was no sunshine afterwards, just a dark ugly sky. That's how he got his name. It was as gray outside as it could be. I looked into his eyes and I knew he was gonna be a handful. It was like he was warning me about what was gonna come. Preparing me for all the shades of gray that he had brought into this world with him. Letting me know that all the love in this world wasn't gonna bring him any sunshine." She sighed again, loosing herself in the memory.

Dr. Burton nodded his head slowly, reaching to take her hand one more time. Together they stood in the window reflecting on the red roses that sparkled beneath the broad daylight and Miss Jen Pearl was thankful for the hand that held on tightly to hers.

SEVEN

Argie Steely, the reporter from the News of Orange County, stood patiently at the foot of the steps waiting for Miss Jen Pearl to retreat from behind her front door. It had taken him well over a week to get her to agree to an interview and he was willing to wait as long as it took to meet with the mother of Graye McAdams, and possibly Graye McAdams himself. He fingered a blue Bic pen between his long fingers and stubbed the toes of his leather boots into the ground, an oversized safari hat sitting slightly askew atop his head. Dressed in a macabre collection of blacks and tans he resembled a distorted character from a Shakespearean play, the aftermath of a really bad literary production. He adjusted his floor length overcoat, the heavy attire out of place in the summer's heat. A list of questions danced quietly in his head as he imagined the editorial accolades a literary coup could yield him.

As Miss Jen Pearl stepped out onto the porch she surveyed him cautiously, noting how the soft in his face suddenly bristled with formality as he pulled himself up from the front step and into character.

Miss Jen Pearl had known Argie since he'd been six years old, pretending to be a swashbuckling pirate at the helm of his own ship. As he pulled at the hairs of his mustache, arched his eyebrows and cleared his throat, she knew that he was still pretending to be something other than the gentle, blue-eyed creature that she knew him to be.

"Good afternoon, Ms. McAdams," he said, lowering the depths of his voice to a deep baritone. "Thank you for seeing me this afternoon."

Miss Jen Pearl shook her head, stifling a giggle. "Argie, since when you take to calling me Ms. McAdams and what's wrong with yo' voice? You catching a cold?"

He shifted slightly. "Ma'am?"

"You heard me. You been calling me Jen Pearl since forever. Now I'm Ms. McAdams and you sounding sickly."

Argie hesitated. "I didn't mean any disrespect Miss Jen Pearl, but since I'm here on business...," his voice trailed as Miss Jen Pearl's gaze stiffened, causing him to drop his own cornflower blue eyes to the floor.

"You means you here to get into my business, don't you?"

"Ma'am, I just want to ask you a few questions about Graye and the murder of Mr. Tate Butler."

"What you need to ask that you don't already know?" Miss Jen Pearl settled herself down onto a metal glider on the porch, gesturing for Argie to take the seat beside her.

"Have you spoken to Graye since the murder?"

"Yes."

"Has he said anything about why he did it?"

"No."

"Do you have any ideas why he might have committed this crime?"

"No."

Argie blew hot breath past his pencil thin lips. Miss Jen Pearl smiled slightly.

"How's yo' mama doing Argie?"

"She's fine, ma'am."

"And yo' sister? What she up to?"

"She's living in Boston, working for a video production company."

Miss Jen Pearl nodded. "You still datin' Miss Henderson's daughter? That pretty little thing with the red hair?"

"Yes ma'am. I'm still with Sarah."

"She a sweet, sweet girl. You done real good."

Frustration furrowed Argie's brow. "Miss Jen Pearl, about Graye..."

Miss Jen Pearl sucked her teeth. "Boy, what about Graye? What you want to know?"

"Is there anything you can tell me about the crime and his participation in it that the general public should know?"

"It was my birthday. Graye took a gun and shot that boy dead. Everyone saw him do it. He's in jail now and there ain't nothin' else to tell." Miss Jen Pearl rose from her seat. "I gots to go get lunch ready fo' Nana Leah now. You come back to see me real soon and bring that girl a yours. I'd like to get to know her better. If you call me first I'll make you a peach cobbler. I remember how much you like my peach cobbler. And tell yo' mama hello for me." The last words fell out of her mouth like hot air from a deflating balloon.

Dismissed, Argie dropped his pen and pad into his lap and sighed as Miss Jen Pearl patted him gently on the shoulder. The contours of his face softened as he watched her retreat back inside, humming softly under her breath as she did. When the door was closed firmly behind her, he rose from his seat and headed for the state penitentiary.

Prison can be hard on a man who isn't himself already hard. The daily ritual of being told who, what, where, when and why, of having one's own personal capacity for thought and emotion squelched could easily destroy a man's spirit. But prison had no effect on Graye. Graye's heart had been frozen in time, his spirit bricked in by his own actions and emotions. Graye was not like other men. Graye had never been like other men.

Graye sat alone in the prison yard, the mid-day sun hot against his skin. Perspiration dripped a trail from pore to pore, sweat forming damp circles against his clothes. Across the courtyard, on the other side of the barbed wired fence, Graye watched as visitors came and went. Mothers, wives, and girlfriends were arriving with bags of goodies for their incarcerated kin. For some odd reason, Graye found that funny and laughed out loud. The inmates who wandered aimlessly around him, barely glanced in his direction, before turning away. The others steered clear of Graye McAdams. It was safer that way.

His name being called over the intercom system interrupted the flow of his thoughts. He could feel himself frowning as he was being summoned to the visitor's room. He was not expecting any visitors. There was no one he wanted to see and no one who he wanted to see him. He rose pensively, sauntering slowly to the inside. At the door of the visitor's lounge, Graye peered through the window, scanning the row of faces that sat behind the insulated glass in anxious anticipation. A guard pushed him lightly, the palm of his hand brushing harshly against the round of his shoulder. Graye glared in response, his hand upon the knob, not wanting to go inside.

"Move it, McAdams."

Graye's eyes narrowed, thin openings against his angry face. "Who's here?"

The guard shrugged. "Look, you got a visitor. So move it or move out. Make a choice."

Graye sucked on his bottom lip, resisting the sudden urge to smash his fist into the guard's face. His body bristled, the muscles along his neck and back tightening.

"I don't need no visitor. Tell them I said so," he muttered defiantly before turning an about face and heading toward his cell.

Dropping onto his cot Graye pulled his knees to his chest. His mind wandered aimlessly, drifting back into time, wishing for days long gone. He yearned for those things now lost to him. As he sat in deep reflection his body quivered ever so gently. He inhaled the rank smell of caged men and the musk that surrounded them. The fumes were putrid as the stench curdled the calm in his belly, threatening to spew the remains of his undigested breakfast onto the floor. The mist of better times and days of youth glistened in the backdrop of his eyes.

Graye wished for a void of silence to fill the noise that stifled his concentration, threatening to invade his calm. He could sense the presence of others, huddled in packs throughout the cell block, too near for any comfort. He sat motionless for hours, refusing to respond when called to dinner, barely flinching when the butt end of a guard's Billy club connected with the side of his body. He sat lost in a memory of darkness.

Graye missed the smell of a crisp spring night, punctuated by the picture-perfect brilliance of a full moon. It was the darkness of night, under the sharp glow of a star-filled sky that gave him an uncanny comfort. He missed the rhythm of evening. He yearned for the dead of night beating a quick syncopation that meshed with the cadence of his heartbeat.

When he was young, he and Tate would pitch a tent in Tate's backyard, wishing that night time would never end. Those were the moments Graye craved for now. He hated having to settle for the sweet memories of them.

"Yo, Tate? You sleep?" Graye's voice rose in a throaty whisper into the cool night air.

"Nah. Just lyin' here watchin' the stars."

"Me too."

Graye allowed the darkness to silence the sound of their voices. Crickets chirped loudly, their song ringing in a dull beat against the damp earth. The air smelled sweet, dew forming droplets against the blades of grass, the green of tree leaves and the sprout of new blossoms awaiting the morning sun. Music billowed from a transistor radio resting on the ground between them, Daryl Hall and John Oates serenading the night with *Rich Girl*.

"Yo, Tate?"

"What?"

"I'm gonna go to New York next week. You wanna come?"

Tate laughed. "You can't go to New York. You ain't but fifteen. You ain't got no money and Miss Jen Pearl will have yo' tail if you up and disappear."

Graye pulled the sleeping bag tightly around his body. "I'm goin'. Got to get out of this town. I'm gonna go crazy if I stay here any longer."

"How you gone get there?"

Graye shrugged his shoulders. "Don't know yet. I'm just goin'."

Tate laughed. As the pitch of his voice rose, the dog at his side rose his head questioningly. Tate reached out to rub his palm against the top of the animal's head.

"What about school?"

Graye ignored the question, turning his attention to the full moon over head. "You ever think about that there moon, Tate?"

"I guess so."

"I'm gone go see that moon one day."

"Uh huh. What you gone do when you get there?"

"Gone just sit and take in all the light. It must be some sort of bright up on that moon."

"Well, then you can't be goin' to no New York. If you gone fly to the moon you need to stay in school so you can learn to be an astronaut. 'Cause you sho' nuff can't walk to no moon!"

It was Graye's turn to laugh, before changing the subject. "You see Stacy Taylor today? Girl looked good. Baby got hips and thighs for days."

"You sweet on Stacy Taylor?"

Graye grunted. "Want some a Stacy Taylor's sweet is what I want."

"You better leave that girl alone. Reverend Taylor be at your mama's door in a heart beat if he even think you tryin' to get next to his daughter."

"His daughter might be trying to get next to me."

"Uh huh."

"You do it yet?"

In the darkness, Tate could feel the color rising into his cheeks. "Ain't yo business."

Graye laughed, flipping his hand in his friends direction. "You weak boy. You still as fresh as the day yo' mama spit you out. Told you what to do to get you some."

"Uh huh."

"I gets me some regular. Be dippin' my lickin' stick in the pudding just like clock work."

"You a lie."

'Who you callin' a lie?"

"Callin' you a lie."

Graye laughed. "You wish I was lyin'. You just jealous 'cause I got somewhere to put my meat. I ain't got to beat it with my left hand."

Tate laughed with him. "No, 'cause you be usin' yo' right."

The dog raised his head once again, looking from his master to the boy on the other side of the tented enclosure. Graye could feel the animal's eyes peering through the darkness at him. "Damn dog be taken notes every time I open my mouth."

Tate chuckled. "Uh huh."

"Should a killed him when I had the chance," he said, rolling over on his side, his back to Tate and the dog.

"You ain't got it in you," Tate whispered back, his fingers entwined deeply into the animal's fur. "You ain't got it in you."

Graye laughed, his eyes closing around the truth. "Now who the one lyin'?" he said. "'Cause we both know that's a lie!"

As Graye continued to chuckle to himself, finding humor where Tate could only see sadness, Stevie Wonder whispered from the radio, *I Wish* dancing into the late night air.

EIGHT

The infant slept comfortably in the bend of Nana Leah's arm as she cradled his fragile frame gently against her body. Those arms had cradled many a baby and this one had fit just as neatly against her chest as all the others. He was a beautiful child she thought to herself as she studied him intently, connecting his features to his family lineage. He looked like his uncles she thought, nodding to herself. Looked just like Jen Pearl's boys had looked when they'd been babies.

His coloring was all McAdams, a warm fusion of red clay and coffee. The full dimpled cheeks and the line of his mouth were all Turrentine, her daddy's people. The gentle curve of his tiny ears was a Mosley trait from her husband Ben's folks. Ben had passed away in 1954, but not before passing them Mosley ears down to Jen Pearl, who'd passed them right along to her own children. The rest of him was his daddy's side of the family. His eyes were a rich amber, an iridescent hue that seemly glowed brighter than sunlight. They were definitely his daddy's eyes. And his hair was his daddy's too. The thick head of auburn waves in striking contrast to the dark, blue-black curls of his mama's people. Nana Leah chuckled softly to herself as the baby shifted in his sleep, stretching the length of his body within her arms.

Nana Leah eased the child up against her shoulder as she rocked her body, and his, in the oversized wooden rocking chair on the front porch. Nuzzling her nose against the top of his tiny head, she inhaled deeply. He smelled like new baby, a sweet freshness blended from talcum powder and innocence. She relished the smell of new baby.

July stood at the bottom of the porch stairs, staring out toward the side yard and the other children who played in the sandbox and swung on the swing set in the play area. Every few minutes she'd break the quiet of Nana Leah's thoughts with the brashness of her voice as she reprimanded someone's child for doing something they weren't supposed to be doing. More often than not it was her own two hellions that she was yelling at.

"Dillon, if you don't stop throwing sand at your brother you better!"

"Lord, child, you about to wear on my nerves yelling at 'dem children. Leave 'dem kids alone. As long as they laughing and screaming you ain't got no cause to worry. Start yelling when one of 'em starts crying 'bouts something."

Miss Jen Pearl laughed as she came out of the house, a pitcher of iced tea and a tray of frosted glasses in hand. "Didn't you just tell her that an hour ago, Mama?"

Nana Leah nodded her head. "Hard headed. Keep looking at me like I don't know what I'm talking 'bouts. Like I ain't raised no babies."

July heaved a deep sigh, rolled her eyes, then returned to her cushioned seat. Lifting a glass to her lips she sipped her sweet tea, the cool liquid refreshing her parched throat. She ignored the duo who sat in the chairs beside her.

Angelette sat against the rail of the top step, quietly watching. She and July exchanged a look between them and the two younger women smiled.

"July, what 'dis baby name again?" Nana Leah asked.

"His name's Kenyan," she responded for the umpteenth time. "Kenyan Tykell Keyes."

"Where you get 'dat name from?" her grandmother asked, her dislike of the choice rolling over her tongue.

July shrugged. "David and I just played around with names that we liked and we liked Kenyan. David's sister came up with Tykell."

Nana Leah turned her attention toward Miss Jen Pearl. "Didn't you teach yo' children that a baby's name had to have some meaning to it. Baby's name supposed to say something 'bout who he is and hopefully who he might become. You don't be picking names like you choosing fruit from some foreign supermarket. Name supposed to be special, not hard to say." She turned back to July. "What's his name again?"

July arched her eyebrows, eyeing her grandmother with visible agitation. "My son's name *is* special thank you very much. What's wrong with Kenyan Tykell?"

Nana Leah cut her eyes in July's direction, patted the baby gently against his back and ignored her comment. Miss Jen Pearl laughed warmly, the sound rising from the depths of her midsection.

Angelette smiled at the exchange. "I think it's a nice name," she ventured, interjecting her opinion into the conversation.

Nana Leah just shook her head, her lips pursed as if she wanted to spit her annoyance.

"Well, what's wrong with it?" July asked again.

"There is nothing wrong with that baby's name," Miss Jen Pearl responded, rocking back and forth in her own chair. "It means something to you and that's all that matters."

"Humph," Nana Leah grunted, the baby jumping slightly in her arms. She ran her thin fingers gently against his bare back, patting her palm against his diapered bottom.

"Young people today be giving they kids some fool names. Shaquita, Chiquita. Gonna have us a whole world of babies named after bananas and ain't no one gone know why."

The women roared with laughter.

Nana Leah ignored their outburst, continuing to speak. "When Jen Pearl was born I took my time naming her. Baby didn't get no name until she was almost eight weeks old. I needed to get to know her some so her name could fit her just right." Nana Leah nodded her head, her eyes darting back and forth from one face to the other as she recalled the memories.

"Once I decided I liked her I wanted her to have a good name. I wanted her named after the things her daddy and I loved best 'cause she was gonna be loved more than anything."

Miss Jen Pearl continued for her. "She named me Jen 'cause yo' grandpa Ben loved his drink more than anything. Gin was his spirit of choice."

The women laughed again.

"But I spelt it pretty," Nana Leah chuckled. "And Pearl came from the very first gift yo' daddy ever give me. Benjamin Mosley give me his mama's pearls on our wedding day. Mama Best, his mama, had been a slave on the old Mosley plantation down by Easton. She got them pearls from Mrs. Hattie Mosley, the master's mama, just before that white woman died. Them pearls was the second greatest present that man ever gave me. I still have them pearls." Nana Leah took a deep breath. "But my baby was the greatest gift Mr. Ben Mosley ever gave me. She was real special and so I gave her a special name that was just right for her - Jen Pearl."

July shook her head smiling. "Angelette, Mama ever tell you about our names?"

Angelette shook her head. "No."

"Tell her, Mama." July rose from her seat to peer over the side of the porch toward the play area. When she was satisfied with what she saw she returned to her seat, turning her attention back to her mother. As she passed Nana Leah and her infant son, she reached a hand out to brush a wisp of hair from the baby's brow.

Miss Jen Pearl shifted in her seat, tapping her fingers easily against the arms of the rocking chair. She smiled slightly, then began to speak.

"I wasn't but fourteen when I met my husband. Lord knows when I met him I swore that was the sweetest man God had put on this here earth. I loved myself some Otis McAdams." Miss Jen Pearl chuckled, blushing slightly. "But Mama wouldn't let me spend no time with him," she said as she cut her eye in the matriarch's direction.

Nana Leah interjected. "Otis won't all that and I didn't have no intentions of you having no babies before you was finished learning something fo' yo' self. But yo' fast tail didn't want to listen. Giving that man your sugar before he'd earned it. I was twenty-five when yo' daddy and I had you. Won't no reason for you be having no babies befo' you was twenty-five."

Miss Jen Pearl shrugged. "Well, I was sixteen when Otis and I snuck off and got married and when we had our first baby, I felt like Otis had given me the best piece of his sugar that he could have ever given me. My baby was the sweetest thing and so I named him Treat. Treat Lee McAdams. Had he been a girl I'd a named her Sugar. Sugar Leah."

Angelette nodded, the smile on her face widening.

Miss Jen Pearl continued. "My next baby was born when we was visitin' Otis' kin in Louisiana. We had to travel past this large lake and the minute I saw all a 'dat water I knew my baby was a girl. There was just something special about that water. It was like it was calling out to me and I made Otis stop so we could eat lunch down by the water side. Baby started coming before we could get back to the house and I had her right there by that water. Didn't know the name of that lake so we just named her Lake. Lake Leah McAdams.

"Now Ginn was named fo' my daddy and fo' me, I guess. Papa passed away the day before she was born. Died with a gin bottle in his hand. That's how she come to be named Ginn Leah McAdams. I just spelt it different from how Mama spelt mine.

"When the twins come here, Treat wasn't but five years old. Lake was 'bout four and Ginn was two. Otis kept tellin' Treat that he was gone get him a baby brother. He just knew this baby was a boy 'cause I was so big when I carried 'em and he spent the whole nine months talking 'bout his "new son this" and his "new son that". Lake didn't want no brother and kept crying 'bout she wanted another sister. Of course every time Lake whined, Ginn whined with her. So when my babies came one right after the other it just seemed to fit to name them what everyone had been calling 'em, Sonn and Sister.

Angelette laughed. Miss Jen Pearl leaned to pull her own glass to her lips, filling her mouth with liquid.

"Do they have a second name?" Angelette asked.

Miss Jen Pearl nodded her head. "Sonn Lee and Sister Leah McAdams."

Nana Leah smiled slightly, nodding her head with a quiet ease.

"In 1955 Otis got himself his first automobile. It was a used Ford pickup truck, but it was one of the prettiest pieces of machinery I had ever seen. Carr was born right in the back of that automobile when we was all comin' back from church one Sunday. I knew he was coming but I thought he'd at least wait until we got home and had Sunday supper. But he was just like that car, too pretty and too fast. Boy still is."

"His second name Lee too?"

July laughed. "What do you think?" she said.

Angelette laughed with her.

"Now my girl July here was supposed to be born in May. I was expecting her around the end of the month. Well, the end of May comes and no baby. Then June and still no baby. Couldn't figure out where I'd got my countin' wrong 'cause here she shows up on the first of July. Just as slow and late as you please. Still like that. Can't depend on her to be no where on time."

July rolled her eyes, raising a hand to fan in her mother's direction.

"So she was named July Leah. Had she come on the fourth I would of named her Sparkle for them fireworks the boys be playing with."

July shrugged her shoulders, raising her eyes in jest.

"My baby August came here right on time. Born one minute after midnight on the first of August. Didn't get no better than that so that's what I named him, August."

Angelette chuckled. "And they all were named after Nana Leah. How come?"

Miss Jen Pearl smiled sweetly, nodding in the direction of her mother. "Cause each one of 'em had Mama's fire in their eyes when they come here. It was like the good Lord had dipped them in her spirit before he sent them to me. Had to name them after her. Didn't have no other choice.

"So how did Graye get his name," Angelette asked softly, her voice dropping to a loud whisper.

Miss Jen Pearl sighed. The air was quiet as she looked out over the yard, listening to the sounds of children playing in the distance. She inhaled deeply, raising the back of her hand to sweep it across her brow. The baby in Nana Leah's lap stirred ever so slightly as though not to disrupt the wave of emotion sweeping over his grandmother. She inhaled again, a deep, mournful breath, held it briefly, then pushed the air past her chapped lips.

"July here was nine years old when Graye was born. Treat had been, what, almost sixteen, seventeen, at the time." She shook her head thinking about it. "I wasn't expecting to have no more babies. What was I supposed to be doing with another baby? Here I was thinking I was going through the change and come to find out I'm pregnant with Graye. Lord have mercy! We was all surprised!" Her head danced from side to side as the recollection flooded through her.

"Now, Graye was difficult from day one. My other babies had been easy to carry, but not Graye. He was just hard on me. The day he was born it was storming something fierce. Didn't have no 'lectricity 'cause the power had blown out, the roads was flooded, and the roof was leaking. It was some sort of mess. When that baby dropped everything was gray. Sky was gray. House was gray. Everybody's mood was gray. And, my baby's eyes were gray. A dull, empty gray. I couldn't find no other name for him. Graye just fit."

Angelette nodded slowly, lost in her own thoughts. "Graye Lee."

"No," Miss Jen Pearl said. "Just Graye. That was all that fit," she finished, tears rising to her eyes. "Just Graye."

The silence was overwhelming, seeming to suddenly engulf them. Angelette stared at her mother-in-law, a quiet understanding passing between them as they thought about the man they both loved so dearly. In the distance the children continued to run and scream in play and the wail of a hungry Kenyan Tykell pulled them back from where the memories had taken them.

NINE

Nana Leah and Miss Jen Pearl waited quietly in the waiting room of Dunn County Regional Hospital. They sat beside four other members from the Faithful Sisters Missionary Board of Holy Trinity Baptist Church. As they did every other Thursday afternoon, they were waiting for the head nurse on duty to tell them that it was okay for them to proceed past the double doors of the hospital's neo-natal care unit. Today, they were waiting for nurse Bernadette Hayes to give that okay. Nana Leah tapped her foot impatiently. Sister Louella Waters smacked a stale piece of chewing gum between her dentures and Sister Ivy Thomas twisted the length of her gray hair around an aged finger. Sister Viola Mae Baker finally broke the silence between them.

"Jen Pearl, how you holding up, Sister? I know it must be a terrible strain on you with all that's been going on with yo' son."

Sister Jasmine Perry pursed her lips, raising her eyebrows with concern. "It's a shame what these young folks will get themselves into these days," she said.

Miss Jen Pearl smiled politely as Nana Leah reached out her hand to pat it against her daughter's knee. The touch, only so gentle, was meant to warn Jen Pearl to be cautious with her response. Her mother would not be embarrassed here in the hospital surrounded by her faithful missionary sisters.

"I'm doing just fine. Thank you for asking, Sister."

Nana Leah leaned forward in her chair. "Everyone's been very supportive. Haven't they daughter?"

"Yes, ma'am." The two women locked eyes, Miss Jen Pearl's annoyance reflecting in her mother's prudish gaze.

Sister Louella clucked her teeth, her ill-fitting dentures snapping like castanets between her gums. "You a good woman, Jen Pearl, to put up with all of Graye's devilment. That boy ain't no good. He would have worn me out years ago," she snapped.

Miss Jen Pearl bit her bottom lip as her mother's nails dug into the thick flesh against her thigh. Nana Leah responded for her, fearing the words that would ease past her daughter's lips were she not to.

"Child done made some bad choices but a good mama doesn't stop loving 'em and doesn't stop being there for 'em. Jen Pearl done been a good mother to Graye. She been a good mother to all of her children." Nana Leah paused, taking a big inhale of air and letting it flow back to the room before preceding. "You ever hear from yo' daughter, Sister Louella?"

Louella bristled ever so slightly. "No, Sister Leah. I don't."

Nana Leah shook her head sympathetically. "Sure 'nuff is a shame that child going off like she done and just leaving dem babies of hers fo' the state to take care of. How many young 'uns did she have, Louella?"

"My Jackie had four. Tisha has two."

"Tisha still got her babies, don't she? I mean wit' that drug problem she had, they didn't take her babies too, did they?"

Sister Louella's ire was raised. "Tisha is doin' fine and so are her children," she responded sorely.

"It's a shame you don't see yo' other grand-kids, Sister Louella. Just a shame." Nana Leah's head continued to bob up and down. Her eyes were bright as she stared deeply into Sister Louella's face. "Being a parent ain't easy these days. Heaven knows we all done had some problems with our children. Just got to keep doing the best we can though. Don't you agree?"

Sister Ivy bobbed her head in agreement. "You are so right, Sister Leah. All we can do is the best we know how."

Nana Leah leaned back in her chair, adjusting the width of her body more comfortably against the plush pillows that folded around her. She and her daughter locked eyes again as Miss Jen Pearl's gaze whispered a silent thank you. Her mother smiled back broadly. She'd said what needed to be said without the bitter intonation that would have spilled out of Miss Jen Pearl's mouth. She knew her daughter's venom could be brutal if not checked and this was not the time for her to be alienating the members of their church.

Silence enveloped them once again as they each drifted off into their own thoughts. As Nana Leah resumed tapping an impatient foot, she focused her thoughts on the small infants that would need the warmth of her arms and just a touch of her heart to lull them with comfort this afternoon. She was grateful when Nurse Hayes finally pushed the doors open and beckoned them inside.

TEN

Graye sobbed. The mournful cries racked the strength of his body, shattering the essence of his spirit. Tears splattered the front of his chambray blue work shirt, running in swells down the round of his cheeks. Across the way, prison authority clothed in masks and gloves, scrubbed the walls and floor of another cell. It had been the last known address for prisoner number JRF9826. The prisoner, an old man formerly known as Manroot Tucker, had taken Graye under his wing the first time Graye had been incarcerated. Each time Graye came back, Manroot had been there to greet him. Each time he left, Manroot had wished him well, imploring him to stay straight. Manroot, serving a life sentence for the murder of his wife, had not wanted to see Graye return, but each time Graye found himself back behind the bars, Manroot had extended his hand in friendship. Manroot Tucker had died in his sleep, just another resident of the state penitentiary. When he died, Graye sobbed. Sobbed like a baby in want of attention.

The guards eyed Graye with reservation. They whispered quietly amongst themselves, never raising their comments loud enough for Graye to hear. But Graye knew what they said. Graye could see the pleasure they took in his anguish. Graye understood their delight over his hurt and still he sobbed. He sobbed not only for Manroot, but also for Tate. The only two friends he'd ever known were lost to him. Graye sobbed for all that was lost to him. Graye sobbed mostly for himself.

Graye had cried often in his lifetime. Usually his tears only fell when he was alone, lost in a darkness of his own making. Graye was comfortable with his tears. Smiling was what he found difficult to do. Graye heaved, sucking in air like a drowning man.

Before, only those he loved most had ever been privileged to see Graye cry. Miss Jen Pearl had seen his tears more times than Graye cared to count. Each and every time he'd been a disappointment to her, Graye had cried an apology. Neither of them ever understood what made Graye do the things he did to hurt his mother so. It was just how it was. It was all either of them had ever known.

Angelette had wiped away his tears only once. The one and only time Graye had gone to the cemetery to visit his Daddy's grave, regret had caused the flow of water to fall. Water had rained down more regret than Graye cared to face. The palm of Angelette's hand had been his tissue that day. Tate had seen him cry often. Tate had seen him cry and had still thought him a man. Tate had never passed judgement. Tate had still called him friend.

Halloween night, Graye and Tate walked the streets picking the best candy out of the bags of children who stood three feet shorter than they did. As Graye picked candy, Tate tried to console each crying child, explaining that Graye was only taking the bad sweets that would rot their teeth. Appeasement had come only after he slipped a few coins into their clenched fists. They'd been seventeen and both knew better. Graye didn't care though and Tate could only do what he knew how to do best. Tate could only think of how to fix it once Graye had broken it.

"You a fool."

"Why?"

"Why you be giving them kids yo' money fo'? You a fool."

"If you wasn't stealing all of their candy I wouldn't have to give them no money."

Graye shrugged, pulling the last piece of a Hershey bar into his mouth.

"They didn't need this candy no way."

Tate could only shake his head. "When you coming back to school?"

Graye shrugged again, lifting his shoulders toward the darkening sky. "Ain't coming" back. Done with school."

"What Miss Jen Pearl say?"

"Didn't tell her yet."

"Hmmm. You in for it now."

"Don't make me no never mind. What she gone do? Beat me?"

"She might."

Graye sucked his teeth. "She might get beat."

"Miss Jen Pearl would wear your ass out if you even thought about lifting your hand to her. Now I know you ain't that crazy." The duo turned down Main Street, heading left toward the center of town.

Graye picked up the pace of their stroll, finished with the conversation. "You going home?" he asked.

"I've got homework to finish. What you gone do?"

"Gone go see the Daniel's sisters. Rose say she got something she want me to see. Say she want to show me her flower garden!"

Tate laughed. "Her flower garden?"

Graye grinned. "That what she say. I told her when we was through I wanted to pluck some fruit from her cherry bush. Girl got all giggly just thinking 'bout it."

Tate shook his head. "You gone get yo' fool self in trouble one day. You sure don't want Miss Hazeline to know you getting with her daughters. Lily was bad enough and now you sniffing after Rose."

Graye laughed loudly, punching his friend playfully in the shoulder. "Want to come see the flowers?"

"Not me. I ain't that stupid."

Graye's body suddenly stiffened. "Who you calling stupid?"

Tate shrugged, quickly noting the sudden swing in the other boy's mood. "Didn't mean nothing by it, Graye."

"You calling me stupid?" The two had come to a dead stop. Graye hovered two inches taller than Tate, the expanse of his body a good four inches wider. Tate stared up into Graye's eyes, the depth of Graye's rage more intimidating than Graye's size had ever been.

Tate smiled slowly, suddenly aware of a hollowness in the pit of his stomach. "We gone fight over this? You know I didn't mean nothin' by it. You know you're not stupid and that I don't think you are. But if we gone fight over it, then that is stupid 'cause you know you can beat my ass and you know I ain't gone fight back. I would be stupid to even think about trying to beat you. So tell me we ain't gone fight over this 'cause I've got to go piss before I wet my pants."

Graye continued to stare his friend down and then just as quickly his mood changed again. He laughed loudly. "You a punk. What would you do without me?"

Tate sighed deeply. "Breathe easier. Why you always got to be messin' wit' me for?

Graye's laughter weakened to a soft chuckle as he turned an about face and continued his walk up the road. "Stupid I guess."

"You know you ain't stupid, Graye. Don't be playing like that. You know you're as smart as anybody out here. Maybe smarter. You just don't want no one else to know it.

Tears suddenly clouded the rim of Graye's eyes. Tate pretended not to notice as his friend swiped at his face with the back of his hand. "Something ain't right with me, Tate. Don't know what it is, but something ain't right."

Tate nodded his head slowly, continuing to stare directly in front of him. Graye's tears had turned from a light mist to a full-fledged storm. Water seeped past his thick dark lashes, dripping down his cheek, past his chin to the ground below. The boy had stopped trying to wipe the telltale signs away with his hand. Instead, he just allowed himself to cry.

The two walked in silence past the closed doors of Miss Hetrick's beauty parlor, the pharmacy, and Dr. Gatewood's dental office. Children had long since headed inside, their nightly antics of dress-up done for another year. The streets were empty, quiet having settled in with the darkness, the sound of Graye's sobs the only discernable noise.

Tate finally responded. "You're who you are, Graye. Ain't for none of us to say if you right or not. You know when you do wrong. You know what you need to do to do right. You're just you. If you need help then me and your mama and everybody will do what we can to get you some help. But you need to help yo' self first. You got to want help, Graye. If you think that there is something wrong with you that needs fixing you got to say so and you got to ask for help. We can't make you." Tate took a deep breath, then finished. "You're my best friend, Graye. I love you like a brother."

Graye wiped the last of his tears from the length of his eyelashes. He nodded his head as he pushed his chest up and out, inhaling deeply. "Right back at 'cha, Tate," he said, pushing his hands deep into the pockets of his denim overalls.

They made the rest of the walk in silence. At the end of the block, without speaking another word, Tate turned toward home and Graye headed for the flowers.

Graye watched as the prison staff finished clearing Manroot's possession's out of the cell. As the heavy bars closed behind them, their footsteps echoing in the distance, Graye continued to sob.

For eight days Graye sat alone in his cell ignoring the daily activity around him. The guards had thought it best to sedate him when on day three he'd lunged at the bars, trying to get at the new prisoner assigned to the cell left vacant by his friend Manroot. The Warden opted not to send him to solitary, an unusually compassionate spirit seeming to understanding the depth of Graye's loss. Instead, Graye was sent to the prison infirmary where a quick visit from the prison doctor, and an injection of Halcion had clouded Graye's pain. Graye was then left to his own devices behind the security of his locked cage.

On day six Graye picked up his leather-bound bible, pulling the heirloom to his chest. He inhaled deeply, taking in the faint aroma of his grandmother's home. He clutched the book tightly, remembering how it had come to be his.

He'd been discarding history as easily as the trash was discarded every Monday and Thursday when the big trucks rolled down the street to retrieve everyone's garbage. The blue-haired woman on the other side of the counter eyed him with disdain as she fingered the delicate pages of the leather-bound bible he'd dropped heavily onto the counter. Photographic images spilled quietly onto the glass top, the captured reflections staring up at Graye with a questioning gaze. The older woman shook her head slowly as Graye tapped his fingers anxiously against his pant leg.

"So, how much you think I can get for this?" he asked, shoving his hands deep into the folds of his oversized jacket.

The woman paused, then sighed deeply before responding. "This bible has been in someone's family for a very long time," she said, gently caressing one of the dropped photos between her thumb and her forefinger. "And the photos. Someone is going to miss these photos."

Graye studied the white woman's wrinkled face as thoughts of his grandmother flashed across his brow. It was Nana Leah's bible that lay before him, the embossed leather casing worn well with age. Too many generations of McAdams' kin had handled that bible, passing it down from parent to child like a valuable life lesson that was not to be lost. And here stood Graye, in Daniel's Antique Shop, trying to get twenty dollars for it to put in his empty pockets.

The woman's disapproving stare told him he was wrong, but he'd known that when he'd stolen it out of the cedar chest at the foot of Nana Leah's bed. He'd known it when the matriarch has asked him for it, tears trickling like rainfall past the crevices of her honey-colored cheeks. He'd pretended to be ignorant of the book's whereabouts as the precious tome lay hidden in the trunk of his brand new 1986 Ford Thunderbird. When she'd asked, he'd lied. Afterwards, he hadn't needed anyone else telling him how wrong he was. His mother had done that, cursing him with every breath she had. But what they didn't understand, Graye thought, was that a moment of necessity sometimes made wrong, right. Right, if only for the moment, and the moment was all Graye was concerned with.

"Well?" asked Graye, annoyance coating the inflection of his words. "What's it worth?"

Mrs. Daniel's picked up the last of the photos and placed them gently back inside the over-sized book. "I can't give you anything for this, Graye. It's not worth anything to me," the woman professed as she picked up the bible and set it carefully into Graye's hands. "You might want to take it back to where you found it," she concluded as she returned to the paperwork on the mahogany desk behind her. "I'm sure it has some value there."

Graye's eyes narrowed as he clutched the bible under his arm. Rage was painted like heavy make-up across his face, the thick lines of anger smeared rouge deep against his flesh. Profanity reverberated in thick swells around the quiet of the room as Graye spewed malice in the woman's direction.

Indifference hung like a veil over her shoulders, shelter from his storm, and when she didn't flinch, not even bothering to raise her eyes, Graye spun his lean frame and the bible in his hands toward the door. It was only when he was outside and the glass door was closed firmly behind him that Mrs. Daniel's lifted her eyes in his direction and sighed.

Three hours later Graye sat on the porch beside Nana Leah, the bible resting in her lap. Neither had spoken since he'd climbed the front steps and had dropped his body into the empty seat at the older woman's side. Even when he'd placed the bible onto the seat between them, an apology caught deep in his throat, Nana Leah had not spoken. Graye sat and watched as she pulled each of the photos from its resting place, studying the images with intense reflection. Every so often the old woman had chuckled quietly to herself.

Miss Jen Pearl had stepped out onto the porch only once to ask if Graye wanted a glass of iced tea and to remind Nana Leah to take her medication. She'd had nothing else to say to either of them.

Just when Graye thought the old woman would never be done, she'd placed the pile of pictures into the pockets of her paisley housedress and turned to look her grandson in the eye. She sighed heavily, reaching a wrinkled hand out to slap the side of his face. Graye had inhaled sharply.

"I'm sorry, Nana," he muttered under his breath, the words wrapping like thick twine around his tongue.

Nana Leah nodded her gray head, running her hand softly against the reddened flesh she'd just struck. "Me too, Baby Boy. Me too." Adjusting the heavy book against her thighs she flipped through the pages, searching the Book of Isaiah until she found the passage she was looking for. As Graye settled back against the cushions of the metal glider, Nana Leah cleared phlegm from her throat, then reached out to take Graye's hand in her own. Her voice boomed past the quiet as she began to read aloud.

"Let the wicked forsake his way, and the unrighteous man his thoughts: and let him return unto the Lord, and he will have mercy upon him; and to our God, for he will abundantly pardon."

Nana Leah rose to her feet, turning to face Graye. "It's yours now," she said, dropping the bible into his lap. "Do right by it and you do right by me and your mother. Do wrong and you do wrong to us all."

Graye smiled at the memory, reflecting on all the words that had said he was headed straight to hell if he didn't change his ways. Graye had no fear of hell. He'd often tiptoed in and out of Satan's playground, lording over the manor with relative ease. It was the door to heaven that Graye feared most, the pearly gates propped just so, waiting to slam close in his face. Heaven held promises he'd never been able to fathom. Promises meant for those who were nothing like him. Opening the yellowed pages, Graye shook the clouds from his head, and began to read.

ELEVEN

Angelette had been eight years old the first time a man put his hands on her. Large, dirty hands sneaking beneath the warmth of her covers to press against her skin. She could vividly recall the panic that consumed her, the fight to distance herself from the hands on her body and the final yielding of a child powerless to beat the hands away. She could easily remember the scream she could not yell, "No, please don't. No," caught in her throat, her tear-filled voice trapped behind the embarrassment and the shame.

Angelette had only been thirteen when her mama's fourth husband, Herman Luther, had stolen her most precious gift. Thirteen years, eight months, and six days to be exact. Like a predator on prey he'd ravaged her innocence, leaving an empty shell of a woman in its place. Too often the memory of the moment would steal Angelette's smile and turn her into someone she could barely recognize.

"You ain't a girl who's meant to be loved," he'd muttered in a drunken stupor. "A girl like you is meant to be fucked. A man would be a fool to love you," he'd pronounced. The words, spewed between the slur of saliva and the bitter of his breath, had dropped like lead weights against her ears. "A man would be a fool not to fuck you," he'd spat. And so he did, trapping her on the stairwell of her mama's home, hemming her into a corner like a caged dog. It had been an ugly act, the assault on her person as vile and as disgusting as one could imagine.

What had hurt Angelette most though was not the bruise between her thighs, but the disregard on her mother's face. Her mother, who professed to love the monster who had violated her daughter so, had labeled her only child a whore. Her mother had looked at her with indifference, her expression alleging that Angelette had somehow deserved what had been done to her. Angelette had believed the look upon her mother's face. Her mother's eyes had been orbs of denial then, unforgiving pools of anger. And though her body had healed, the physical pains fading into oblivion, Angelette still nurtured the scar left by the memory of what she had seen in her mother's eyes.

It would be many men later, well after Herman Luther, when she would continue to ask what kind of man would shatter the dreams of an eight-year-old with his filthy hands. Angelette was still desperate for sleep that could not be disturbed. She hated the hands that could shatter her dreams in the middle of the night. She begged to know what kind of man, the answers lost somewhere behind a mother's stare.

For as long as Angelette could remember men had always looked at her with panting eyes. Eyes like those of Herman Luther. Angelette imagined they saw what he had seen, what he'd taken pleasure in showing her mother. In her mind it was not the satiny, butter-toned skin, or the dark intensity of her feline eyes, or the sweet, delicate lines of her full lips that they saw. It was not the intoxicating beauty which had been her birthright that they paid homage to or the elegance that danced the length of her curvaceous frame.

To Angelette, it was her ugly that they saw. It was the ugly of having been birthed in a field full of bitter and hate. It was the ugly of having been bottle fed sonnets of malice and jealousy and never having dined on poetry that rang of love and wanting. It was the ugly of being thought brainless and hopeless and without spirit; of being seen as nothing more than nicely packaged meat to be used, and used again, until there was nothing else left to use.

It was the ugly reflected in the panting eyes that told Angelette her only value lay beneath the mound of pubic hair between her legs. It was the ugly that whispered she was not meant to be loved. That was the image that peered back at Angelette when she looked in the mirror. It was the image reinforced on her fifteenth birthday when her mama disappeared with husband number five, another husband who'd looked at Angelette with panting eyes.

Angelette had been just three weeks shy of her sixteenth birthday when Graye had come rushing into her life like a summer rain, much needed moisture after a long period of drought. His pale, brooding eyes had been different from all the others. He'd been different and so Angelette had latched on to Graye like an infant latches on to a pacifier, refusing to let go.

It was Christmas Eve, December 1995, and where most people had gone home to family or friends to celebrate, Angelette and Graye had gone to the Easy-Slide Café. The local bar had only been open because Graye had slipped a hundred dollar bill into Leander Hampton's pocket for a few extra hours of the man's time.

The Commodores played in the distance, fortified by a roll of quarters Graye dropped into the jukebox. Graye had been in a rear corner nodding his head in time to the music, nursing the empty shot glass in his hand. Angelette had eased inside searching for warmth.

Graye watched Angelette as she made her way to the bar, her arms wrapped around her shoulders. Leander's face was expressionless as he rinsed soapy water from a newly washed glass. Graye wondered why the girl whispered as he watched Leander lean in closer, trying to hear what she was saying. Graye's eyes darted from her to him and back again trying to guess at the words being exchanged. Still drying the glass in his hand Leander only nodded his head up and down, gesturing for her to take a seat. The girl crossed over to one of the tables and sat down. Lining the glass up beside the others he'd just finished drying Leander came from behind the bar and headed toward the kitchen. He raised an eyebrow in Graye's direction as he passed, tossed a glance toward the girl, then turned his head back to Graye and winked. Graye nodded as though some unspoken message had passed between them. He reached for his bottle and poured the fluid into his empty shot glass. Without missing a beat, he swigged the bitter fluid down in one gulp, wiping his mouth against the back of his hand before setting the glass back down onto the table.

Occasionally the girl would glance toward Graye, but would quickly drop her eyes back to the table when she caught him staring boldly. Graye found her actions almost comical as she rocked slowly in her chair, her arms still clutched across her chest. She was pretty he thought to himself as he studied her carefully. Almost too pretty with her cat-like eyes and caramel complexion he thought. He couldn't tell by the clothes she wore, but he imagined her to have a decent figure. Her clothes did not fit her properly though, oversized denim jeans and a man's plaid flannel work shirt beneath a too small trench coat. The clothes were as out of place on her body as she was out of place in the room.

Leander returned with a ham and cheese sandwich, a slice of his wife's lemon pound cake, and a cup of coffee, setting the tray carefully in front of her. Graye leaned back easily in his chair to watch the young girl eat. He was even more amused as he watched her devour the sandwich, barely chewing each bite before swallowing. She was starved and she ate like she'd not eaten in days.

From where she sat Angelette could feel him staring, studying her every move. She'd grown accustomed to men staring at her and so she wasn't concerned about him watching her so brazenly. She'd learned at a very early age how to ignore a man who watched her too closely.

The food was good and she was hungry. She was also cold and the chill through her body was just beginning to thaw as she sipped at the hot cup of coffee the bartender had brought her. This moment wouldn't last long she thought. Before too long she'd have to return to the streets and the cold and the loneliness that had become a constant companion since her mother had left. It would be another long bus ride to another town she didn't know, hoping to find just a little piece of something she could call her own. The cold she could handle. The loneliness though had almost become too much to bear. She craved companionship that didn't have to do with someone putting their hands on her. All she wanted was someone to talk to, someone who wanted to talk to her. She glanced up again toward the man on the other side of the room.

As Angelette locked eyes with Graye and held the gaze, the man nodded his head slowly. Angelette smiled shyly, a quick bend of her lips that seemed to cushion the soft lines of her face. Graye took it to be an invitation as he lifted his large body from the chair and his glass and bottle from the table. Making his way to where Angelette sat, he planted himself in the chair across from her and poured another drink. As Angelette held out her coffee cup Graye poured the last of his bottle into the black of the coffee that settled against the bottom. Neither said a word, the only conversation between them being carried by their eyes. Graye continued to watch her as she finished the last of her pound cake, dabbing at the plate with a moistened finger to catch all the crumbs. He smiled sweetly.

"You want more?" he asked, speaking out loud for the first time. He gestured for Leander who came with her bill in hand.

Angelette shook her head. "No, thank you. I've had enough," she purred, the thick of her voice a rich satin that seemed to warm Graye from the inside out. He smiled, a wide grin that spread from the depths of his insides to the curvature of his face.

As the girl fumbled in her pockets, Graye lifted his hand in her direction. "Don't worry about it. It's on me," he said, dropping a twenty-dollar bill onto the table.

Angelette clutched at the empty lining of her coat pocket. She'd not had any money to pay with any way and so she smiled her sweetest smile, the one that men seemed to fawn all over her for. Graye laughed loudly.

Leander stood beside them watching the duo with interest. "I'm ready to close up, McAdams. It is Christmas Eve."

Graye extended his arm and the two men shook hands warmly. "Appreciate it, Leander. I owe you one."

"Merry Christmas," the man responded, looking at Angelette as he did. "Wish Miss Jen Pearl a happy holiday for me," he said to Graye, passing the younger man his overcoat.

Graye nodded as he pulled on the brown wool garment. He turned toward the door. The girl still sat at the table watching him as he made his way toward the exit. The smile had faded from her face. Graye glanced back, then hesitated.

"You got somewhere to stay?"

Angelette shook her head. "No."

"Come on then," he said, gesturing for her to follow him.

Angelette sighed deeply, throwing a glance toward Leander who nodded his head as if giving her permission. Angelette sighed again as she got up to follow behind Graye. The other man smiled and waved as he called out "Merry Christmas" behind the two of them. "You take care of that child, Graye," he added, more for his own benefit than hers.

Outside, Graye pulled his coat closer, bracing himself against the cold chill that twisted through the air. He watched the girl and she watched him. Pointing toward the west side of town he gestured for her to follow. The walk was cold and neither spoke as Angelette raced to keep up with Graye's long strides. As he crossed through people's yards, stopping only to wave if someone looked out a window or to curse a barking dog, Angelette began to wonder if she should be scared. Although the man seemed to be okay there was something about him that made her nervous. Something that made her stomach muscles tense ever so slightly.

As they made a final turn onto a dirt road and crossed over the yard Graye finally spoke. "You can sleep in my bed. I'll sleep on the couch. Tomorrow we'll go over to my mama's for Christmas. She lives over there, across the way." He pointed toward the darkened house that stood in the shadows on the other side of the road, then turned to stare down at her. "Okay?"

Angelette looked up into the gray of his eyes, the color highlighted by the streetlight they stood beneath. She reached a hand to brush the hair out of her face and smiled weakly, nodding her head in response. Inside the small, white house, Graye lit a fire in the fireplace as he rambled on about his mother and grandmother who lived across the way and the family that would be there tomorrow to celebrate the holiday. He talked and Angelette listened. When he tossed her an old tee shirt to change into she blushed slightly, embarrassed that she didn't even have a change of garments to put on her body. Graye nodded his head as though reading her thoughts. "Don't worry 'bout it. I'll get you some clothes from my mama tomorrow."

Behind the curtain that Graye had drawn close, Angelette dropped her jeans and flannel top to the floor, pulling the tee shirt over her white cotton bra and striped pink panties. On the other side of the curtain Graye stripped down to his briefs and dropped the length of his dark body against the sofa, pulling a woolen blanket up and over his legs.

Inside the small bathroom Angelette welcomed the warmth of water that washed over her face and hands. Graye smiled as he heard her humming softly to herself. Minutes later, tucking the covers around her body Angelette fell into the sag of the mattress, molding her body into the curve that usually held Graye's large frame. She was suddenly tired and just before succumbing to the sleep that called out to her, she sat upright, drawing her knees to her chest.

"Thank you," she said calling out to where Graye lay, the faint line of his body etched in the darkness.

The man nodded. "Don't worry about it."

"What's your name?"

"Graye. Graye McAdams. What's yours?"

"Angelette."

Graye paused before speaking. "Angelette...that's a pretty name. I like that name."

The girl smiled. "Merry Christmas, Graye."

"Yeah, Merry Christmas. Merry Christmas, Angelette."

TWELVE

Surprise rang warmly in her voice as he greeted her over the other end of the telephone. He could hear the rising excitement in the inflection of her words and though he would never admit it, he was as anxious to hear her voice as she was to hear his. The guard standing at his elbow and the other inmates waiting their turn behind him could not read his joy at knowing his woman was still there, still wanting him as much as he wanted her. They would never know the compulsive need he felt for Angelette.

"Are you alright?" Angelette asked, not having been prepared to hear Graye's voice on the other end of the receiver. "Are they treating you well?"

Grey smiled. "It's prison, Baby Doll. It can't never be alright." They both sighed. "You doin' okay without me?"

Angelette hung her head. "I'm fine. Yo' mama's doing okay, too. She worries about you though."

Graye could feel his throat tightening, tears starting to puddle under the lids of his eyes. He shook the emotion to the floor, turning to glare at another inmate who'd bumped into him. His eyes told the man to watch himself. He didn't trust his voice to convey the same tone and so he said nothing, just squinted his eyes in anger and clenched the fist at his side. The man, a tall ebony brother with bad skin and a too large afro sucked his teeth, flipped Graye his middle finger, then retreated off to the side, turning his back. Graye pointed his index finger in the man's direction to indicate it wasn't over. Graye wasn't done with him. He was going to have to pay. It was a matter of respect. Respect behind those iron bars was all Graye had and he couldn't afford to lose it.

"I gotta go Angelette. I just wanted to check on you. I need you to send me some stuff too."

"What you need?"

"Need me some new sneakers and a couple cartons of cigarettes. Need 'em soon too. You hear me?"

"Yes, Graye, I'll take care of it right now."

"I miss you, Angelette. "

Angelette nodded into the telephone.

Graye lowered his voice, clutching at the receiver in his hand. "You heard me, Angelette?"

Angelette whispered, her voice barely audible. "Yes, Graye."

"You still love me don't you, Angelette?" She could hear the subtle plea in Graye's tone. "You still do, don't you?" he asked again.

Tears rolled down the line of Angelette's face, settling on the front of her white cotton blouse. She swallowed hard before responding. "Always, Graye. No one but you."

Graye sighed, the smile returning to his face. "Me too, Baby Doll. Get my stuff for me and I'll talk to you soon. I gotta go now."

"Bye, Graye."

"Bye, Baby Doll."

Two hours later, after a stern lecture from the Warden, Graye was put into solitary confinement for having assaulted another inmate with a blunt instrument. Graye had beaten the man unconscious with a telephone receiver he'd pulled out of the wall. The man's skull had been fractured and his nose and jaw broken. Graye had gone easily, entering the confines of the six by six enclosure as naked as the day he was born. When the guard closed the heavy iron door, shutting out the light, Graye sank quietly to the floor, curling the length of his body into fetal position. Graye made himself comfortable knowing he was going to be there for a good while. But Graye was use to isolation. Graye didn't mind the time alone.

The minutes ticked away into hours and before too long the hours became days. Graye drifted in and out of sleep, his mind tottering on the brink of insanity. Graye had always hung precariously on the edge of crazy and he was comfortable there. It was just how he was. He kept thinking of Angelette, dreaming about her. He thought he felt her once, her hand running up the length of his leg. In his mind she'd been very real and that was all Graye needed to help him pass the time away.

Christmas Eve 1995 had been the beginning. He and Angelette had found each other at the Easy-Slide Café. They'd been together ever since. He knew when he'd taken her home to his mama's Christmas Day that Angelette was what he needed. Angelette would keep him from falling completely off the edge.

He'd risen early, slipping into the same clothes he'd worn the night before. The clock at the side of his bed read four-fifteen. In his bed, the girl slept soundly. Graye picked her clothes up off the floor and tossed them into the basket with the rest of his dirty laundry. He watched her as she lay wrapped around his pillows, her mouth open ever so slightly, morning breath blowing past her lips. The blankets had fallen off the side of the bed exposing her legs and backside. The tee shirt was pushed up around her arms and Graye could see the round of her breasts pressing into the mattress. Her skin reminded him of thick caramel and he couldn't help thinking about how sweet she just might be. He wanted to touch her, to taste her honey, but he resisted the urge. As she stretched ever so slightly Graye was reminded of just how young she was. He disregarded the rising sensation in his groin. Picking up the lost covers he tossed them back over her body before heading across the street to see his mother.

Miss Jen Pearl was in the kitchen when Graye entered the house. The cooking had already begun and Graye inhaled the sweet essence of cinnamon and sugar, the spices floating thickly in the air. Miss Jen

Pearl's hands were lost inside the inner cavity of a large turkey as she filled it with her famous pecan stuffing. She smiled at her son as he poured himself a cup of dark coffee and took a seat at the table.

"Merry Christmas, Graye."

"Merry Christmas, Mama."

"We missed you last night. Had us some fish for dinner. I saved you a plate."

"Sorry."

Miss Jen Pearl studied him momentarily. "What you need, Graye?" she asked, sensing a question hanging on Graye's tongue.

"You got any of Ginn or Sister's old clothes I can have?"

Miss Jen Pearl rinsed her hands off, then slid the turkey into the oven. "What you need them girl's clothes for?"

"Just somethin' fo' my new friend to wear to supper tonight and some clean underclothes if you have 'em."

"What friend is this?"

Graye met his mother's gaze with his own, the woman's eyebrows raised questioningly. "Her stuff got stolen at the bus station," he said, "and she don't have nuthin'. She gone stay with me for a while and she need something just fo' today. I'm gone go buy her some new clothes tomorrow when the store open back up. Her name's Angelette."

Miss Jen Pearl nodded her head. Graye had volunteered more information than she expected and so she didn't push him for more. "Watch my stove fo' me. Don't let my sauce burn. That's my cheese sauce for the broccoli."

"You makin' my casserole, Mama?"

Miss Jen Pearl reached up to kiss her son on the forehead as she passed by. "Sweet 'tata casserole already done, baby."

Graye grinned as his mother headed down into the basement. Sipping the hot fluid he welcomed the warmth that traveled down his throat into his midsection. It was a good cup of coffee. The pot on the stove bubbled and Graye rushed to turn down the burner. Stirring the thick blend of cheddar, Swiss, and American cheeses, Graye watched as it coated the silver of the spoon. Graye inhaled the pungent aroma. He loved the smell of his mother's kitchen. Cooking aromas that seeped into your pores and filled your soul even before the food filled you stomach.

Angelette would get a real good meal this afternoon. His thoughts of the girl were interrupted as his mother made her way back up the stairs.

Miss Jen Pearl lifted her aching knees up the last of the steps. "Your lucky day, Graye," she said, dropping the clothes she carried into his arms. "I found two nice dresses, a pair of slacks, three sweaters and a brand new pack of cotton panties Sister ain't never opened."

Graye smiled. "Thanks, Mama."

Miss Jen Pearl nodded her head. "If they fit her tell yo' friend to just keep 'em all. Them girls ain't never gone get back in them clothes."

Graye nodded.

Miss Jen Pearl continued. "You got somethin' to feed her fo' breakfast 'cause if you don't there's some sausage and biscuits on the counter and some orange juice in the fridge. Take that back with you and give the girl something to eat." Miss Jen Pearl paused to take a breath as she moved the cheese sauce to the back of the stove. She lifted a clean pot filled with water to the already hot burner. "We gone eat dinner at three o'clock Graye so don't you and yo' friend be late. You hear me?"

Graye continued to nod his head as he wrapped some food in aluminum foil and pulled the bottle of juice from the refrigerator. "We'll be here, Mama." Graye reached out to hug his mother, swallowing her body in the cavity of his arms. "I love you, Mama."

Miss Jen Pearl shook her head as she watched Graye make his way back across the street, a brown bag filled with old clothes in one hand, a plate of sausage and biscuits in the other. This girl must be special Miss Jen Pearl thought to herself. Graye had never before bought any woman home for them to meet and here he was bringing this girl for Christmas dinner. Turning back to her stove Miss Jen Pearl pushed thoughts of Graye out of her head as she went back to preparing the holiday meal.

The sound of the metal door opening pulled Graye away from his memory. "Breakfast," a voice called out before sliding a metal plate across the floor in his direction. Graye shielded his eyes from the sudden flash of light that blinded him. The plate slammed into his leg, spilling some of its contents across the floor. Graye wasn't interested in the slop they served him and so he pushed the plate back in the direction that it had come from. The guard shrugged, picked the tin container up and slammed the door closed again.

Graye rolled back onto his side cradling his head with his arm. Angelette had smiled when he'd given her those clothes, a wide grin that had radiated from her midsection.

No one had ever given her anything before. As she nibbled on a biscuit and sipped at the juice, Graye ran a tub full of warm sudsy water for her to bathe in.

"We having dinner at Mama's."

She nodded. "Is that gone be okay? She won't mind me being there will she?"

Graye smiled. "Mama would be mad if you didn't come 'cause I told her I was gone bring you."

Angelette brushed the crumbs from her lap and lifted her thin body from the bedside. As Graye watched she pulled the white tee shirt up and over her head, then unsnapped her brassiere. His eyes followed the white fabric as it dropped to the floor, then scanned up the length of her body. He inhaled sharply as she pulled at her nipple with two fingers. She had beautiful breasts. Angelette walked toward Graye, her eyes focused on the tops of his shoes. When she stood directly before him she lifted her gaze to look into his eyes.

"I don't have no present to give you fo' Christmas and you been so nice to me..." She paused, her words dropping off like a feather hitting the floor.

Graye cleared his throat, dropping his hand to his crotch. The fabric of his pants was pulled tightly against a rising erection. With his other hand he reached out to stroke the side of Angelette's breast with the flat of his palm. He inhaled deeply as Angelette flinched ever so slightly. Taking two steps back Graye dropped both of his hands back down to his sides.

"That water gone get cold if you don't hurry up." His voice was low, his tone soothing.

Angelette stood awkwardly. "I'm sorry," she said, crossing her hands over her chest. "I didn't mean to..."

Graye smiled, shaking his head from side to side. "Don't you worry 'bout no present for me. Just go get ready, okay?" He wiped his palms against his pant leg.

Angelette smiled broadly, heading for the bathroom. When she was settled comfortably in the tub, Graye closed the door between them. As he stood with his forehead pressed against the door, listening to the rustle of water on the other side, he slowly stroked the tension out of his crotch.

The memory of Angelette's body lengthened the line of an erection and Graye cursed under his breath. Pulling himself upright he slid across the floor until his back hit the wall. Blood continued to surge through his penis as Graye wrapped the palm of his hand around his privates. Only Angelette knew how to soothe the beast that was consuming him Graye thought. Only Angelette, and Angelette wasn't there. Graye hurled a path of expletives into the rank air, still stroking the length of his manhood. Graye's falling off the edge of sanity is what was keeping them apart now he thought. Images of Tate Butler flashed before his eyes and when he thought of Tate lying face up, blood seeping from his chest, his erection died.

Still holding the limp flesh in his hand Graye fell over onto his side, his mind tap dancing right on the fringe of madness.

THIRTEEN

Doctor Horace Burton escorted Miss Jen Pearl and Angelette to Tate Butler's funeral. Miss Jen Pearl had considered making the whole family attend, but had figured too many McAdams' would have made the Tate family uncomfortable. When Miss Jen Pearl extended her arms, Tate's mama had hesitated ever so slightly before allowing the woman to wrap her in a hug. The two held onto each other tightly, the beat of their hearts rising and falling in perfect unison. No words were exchanged between them, just the warmth of one mother being passed to another, both having suffered a loss that would stay with them until the end of their days.

The service was well attended. Tate had been much loved in their small community. His mother and his ex-wife held hands at the front of the church as Tate's eight-year-old daughter hung awkwardly beside them, trying to make sense of the season. Angelette had leaned to kiss the round of the child's cheek, wanting to tell her something profound. Having no words whatsoever to share, she could only wipe a tear from the child's eyes and a tear from her own.

On the ride home Miss Jen Pearl had gone unusually quiet. Dr. Burton rattled on and on, trying to make conversation. Angelette wasn't sure what to say or if she should say anything at all. Miss Jen Pearl seemed to ignore them both, never bothering to respond when Dr. Burton asked if she'd like to stop for some ice cream since they weren't going back to the Tate home to sit with the family. Even when he pulled into the parking lot of Honey's Diner on the corner of Umstead and Duke Streets, Miss Jen Pearl barely seemed to notice.

Angelette waited quietly by the front door of the restaurant as Dr. Burton helped Miss Jen Pearl out of the car and walked her to the door with one arm around her waist and the other clasped tightly to her hand. For the very first time Angelette noticed how fragile her mother-in-law seemed.

Once they were seated at a back booth in the no smoking section, Dr. Burton ordered chocolate sundaes for each of them, with extra whipped cream and extra cherries. As the waitress sat the overflowing plates of confection in front of them

Angelette suddenly felt like a little kid in a candy shop. It was the first time she'd ever felt like a little kid and the emotions were overwhelming. She couldn't help but giggle as the abundant dish of ice cream and color-filled condiments jiggled in oblivion before them.

When the first wave of laughter consumed her, Angelette was horrified, her eyes searching Miss Jen Pearl's face for some indication that she'd committed a horrendous faux pas by laughing so unabashedly just minutes after weeping over Tate's dead body. But her rising laughter seemed to draw Miss Jen Pearl back to the conversation and the older woman suddenly laughed with Angelette. Dr. Horace Burton smiled his approval.

"Did I get it right, Jen Pearl," he asked, leaning his shoulder up against the woman's. "Did they put enough whipped cream and cherries on top?"

Miss Jen Pearl smiled as she pulled a spoonful of cold silk into her mouth. "My husband Otis bought me my first ice cream sundae. Otis loved himself some ice cream."

Dr. Burton nodded his head approvingly. "Otis loved a lot more than ice cream. " He pulled his own spoon of cold mush to his face. "What Otis loved was anything that bought a smile to your face. That man loved to see you happy." Dr. Burton nodded his head as he continued. "I remember how Otis used to hang on to everything you did and said. Didn't want anyone else to get too close to you either. That man would cut right up if he thought someone was getting too close to his Jen Pearl."

Miss Jen Pearl cut her eye toward Dr. Burton, then shrugged her shoulders. "Otis was no different from most men who think everything you are and everything you have belongs only to them."

Angelette looked at Miss Jen Pearl. "Like Graye?"

Miss Jen Pearl held the spoon against her tongue, relishing the cool metal within her mouth as she pondered Angelette's question. Dr. Burton responded for her, the words rushing past his thin lips before his mind had an opportunity to form a proper answer.

"Just like Graye. His daddy loved Jen Pearl just like Graye loves you. It's that kind of love that can scare you if you don't understand it. It's that type of love that can hurt terribly if you don't know how to control it. Graye is just like his daddy that way. Just like his daddy was." Dr. Burton's head bobbed up and down on his thin neck like a loose hinge.

Miss Jen Pearls sighed, finally nodding her own head in agreement. Her eyes met Angelette's. "Graye is more like his daddy than any of my other children ever was. None of my other boys have ever lived as hard or loved as hard as Otis did. Only Graye. Only my Graye."

"Daddy Otis ever hurt you the way Graye has hurt me?" Angelette seemed to whisper the question, leaning across the table toward Miss Jen Pearl as the words fell into the melting mess in front of her. "Did he ever hurt you bad like that?"

The two women locked eyes. Dr. Burton could feel Miss Jen Pearl start to tremble ever so slightly and he rested his palm against the curve of her arm. The tenderness of his gesture seemed to help her find the answer that Angelette was desperate to hear.

"Otis didn't always do right, but not all men know how. I wanted what Otis wanted and that worked for us. He wasn't an easy man to deal with but he loved me and he loved our children. We came first with each other, always. It doesn't hurt when you know that's what you want. It's like Doc here said. It only hurts when you don't understand it and don't know how to control it. And it can kill you when it's not what you both want."

Angelette nodded her head, her eyes darting back and forth in deep concentration.

Miss Jen Pearl smiled, pushing the empty dish toward the center of the table. "Dr. Burton here won't much different from Otis or Graye. He loved his wife just as much. Was just as jealous over her too. Don't think that he won't." She elbowed her friend affectionately.

Dr. Burton laughed. "Now I'm just jealous over Jen Pearl when she let me be."

Miss Jen Pearl blushed. "You hush yo' mouth, you old fool.

Angelette laughed with them, running her forefinger along the metal dish to catch the last of the syrupy sweetness in her bowl.

A wave of sadness suddenly crossed Angelette's face as she reached out to take Miss Jen Pearl's hand. When she finally spoke, her voice was barely a faint echo above the piped in piano music, the hollow of her words bringing tears to Miss Jen Pearl's eyes.

"It's all my fault. Graye should never have loved me so much. It wasn't supposed to be like this."

Dr. Burton clasped her other hand beneath his own. "Why not Angelette? Why wasn't Graye supposed to love you so much?" he asked.

"'Cause I didn't know how to love him back. No one had ever taught me how to love any man that hard."

Miss Jen Pearl sat in the shadows of darkness, not wanting to turn on any lights in the small bedroom. On the other side of the wall, where her room bordered Nana Leah's, she could hear the woman humming loudly, humming a hymn to lull herself into sleepiness. Jen Pearl rocked slowly, waving her body back and forth as she sat propped on the edge of the high bed. She'd managed to kick her low, black heels off and had pulled down the length of her pantyhose, but she'd not yet bothered with the dress, the black silk mourning garment feeling comfortable against her skin.

The first time she'd worn the dress had been at Otis' funeral. She'd worn it to dozens of others since, but she'd worn it for Otis first. She remembered how she and the girls had gone shopping for clothes to wear to their daddy's funeral, all of them crying like babies as they sifted through the racks. It was the first time she'd bought silk, deciding that sending her husband home to meet his maker required something more than simple cotton. Jen Pearl ran her hand down against the length of her thighs, a dull smile forming as she relished the sensation of the fabric against the palm of her hand. Otis would have liked the feel of silk.

Angelette had awakened her memories of Otis. Memories that she'd not wanted to ever recall. Not everything about Otis had been good and the day she'd planted him in the ground, lying his body in the same plot where she would one day lay, she had promised herself to only remember the good things about Otis McAdams. The rest of it was best left with the dead. Now Angelette had summoned those memories back from the afterworld and they'd risen like haunted spooks to betray her.

The quiet of her home was broken by Otis McAdams screaming her name as he came through the front door. Two-year-old Treat played happily at the foot of the chair she sat in. Her infant daughter, Lake, lay nursing at her breast, suckling against a bruised nipple. Both children jumped, startled from their contentment, the baby's disturbance causing her to break out in a frightful wail. Jen Pearl rocked the crying child, her own anxiety causing her baby daughter further distress. Otis screamed again.

"You hear me calling you!" the man shouted loudly, the volume of his voice loud enough to wake the dead.

"What's wrong, Otis?" Jen Pearl asked, coming to her feet as she shifted the young child against her shoulder and adjusted the front of her housecoat.

Otis continued to scream. "I been outside calling for you for ten minutes now!"

"I didn't hear you, Otis. I was feeding the baby."

The man shook his finger in her face, stepping closer as he hissed past clenched teeth. "I'm tired a 'dis. Tired a working all damn day and you ain't doing nothing here in this house to help out."

"What's wrong, Otis? What didn't I do? I was just trying to feed the baby."

The man's stare was venomous. "Forget it."

"Forget what, Otis? I still don't know what you yelling about." Jen Pearl reached down for Treat's hand, the young boy staring nervously from her to his father and back again. He gripped her fingers tightly, leaning to hide his face against the back of her leg. Pulling him behind her, she led him out of the kitchen to the bedroom.

"Treat, you be a good boy and watch Lake for Mama, okay?"

Large, wide eyes stared up at her, a thick head of crinkled curls bobbing up and down.

"You sit right here on the bed with the baby and pat her easy on the back so she go to sleep. Mama will be right back," she finished, kissing him on the forehead as she hugged him tightly.

"I scared, Mama," he said, his bottom lip trembling with fear.

"Hush now," Jen Pearl said, "You ain't got to be scared a yo' daddy. He just tired is all. Now watch Lake for me like a good boy."

As she exited the room, Treat was still shaking his head up and down against his shoulders.

Otis sat at the kitchen table, leaning to pull his mud-caked work boots off his swollen feet. He cut his eye at her, but said nothing, kicking dirt from his pant leg to her freshly washed floor.

"How was yo' day?" Jen Pearl asked sweetly, reaching for a plate on the counter and filling it with food.

"How you think it was? I worked hard, that's how it was. Worked hard so you can spend all my money on nothing. Worked hard so you can keep me in the poor house."

"How do I spend all yo' money?"

Otis sucked his teeth. "I don't see none a it. Ain't got nothing to show for it. Nothing."

"You has two babies who ain't hungry, and a house with a good roof, and a woman who loves you. What more do you want?" Jen Pearl asked, ire rising in the tone of her voice.

Otis rolled his eyes.

"You ain't never happy Otis, never."

"You don't do nothing to help, either does you?" he barked. "When you gone get a job?"

"What I'm gone do with these babies if I go to work?"

"Yo' mama will look after 'em."

"I'm their mama. I'm supposed to look after 'em."

"You need to help pay some of these damn bills."

"Well, if I have to do that, then what do I need you for?"

Otis bristled, slamming a fist against the table. "That's right. You don't need me, do you. Ain't that what you said. You can do it by yourself if you have to."

"Why are you being so ugly, Otis? Why? What did I do for this?"

"I'm sick a 'dis and I'm sick a you."

"What you sick of, Otis? You sick a me cooking breakfast, packing yo' lunch, making sure your dinner's on the table the minute you get home? Are you sick a me washing yo' clothes and cleaning yo' house? You sick a me looking after yo' children? You sick a me lying in that bed any time you want me? Just what is it about me that makes you so sick, Otis McAdams? Please tell me."

In the other room she could hear both Lake and Treat crying softy. She winced, angrier now because her babies were crying and there had been no reason for it. She dropped a plate of fried chicken, stringbeans, macaroni and cheese, and hot rolls onto the table in front of her husband. "This ain't right, Otis. This ain't right," she said, dropping her voice to an angry whisper.

"There gone be some changes, Jen Pearl. I ain't putting up with this much longer."

"Fine. Do what you have to do."

Silence wafted between them as they stood staring intently at each other. Jen Pearl heaved a heavy sigh. "I've got to go put the babies to bed."

Otis nodded his head. "I'm making work early. Got to be at the plant by four o'clock in the morning."

"Yo' food'll be on the stove. I'll pack yo' breakfast and yo' lunch for you."

"I'm going to bed early, too. Want me some nookie so I can go to sleep. Don't keep me waiting."

Jen Pearl dropped a hand to her hip, her look incredulous. She shook her head.

"Don't look at me like that," Otis said, pulling a piece of meat to his lips. "You need to take care of yo' business."

"And what if I don't want to?"

The man shrugged. "Then lay there like you usually do. Don't make no difference to me."

"My body could be dead cold and it wouldn't make you no never mind, would it, Otis?"

"Oh, I mind it, but since you don't put no effort in it, there ain't nothing I can do."

"Otis, this ain't..."

"Shut up," Otis said, interrupting. "I don't want to talk about it no more. You got to talk things to death. You can't do nothing I ask. Got to have things yo' way all the time. Ain't happy if you ain't in control. Well, I'm gone say this time. I'm in control and I'm sayin' I don't want to talk about it no more."

Jen Pearl closed her eyes, the sounds of her children pulling at her. Opening them up again, she stared at Otis McAdams, his attention now focused on his dinner. His gaze fell somewhere right past her, as if she weren't even in the room. Turning on her heels, Jen Pearl rushed to comfort her babies, before it would be time to have to make Otis McAdams happy.

Faint shadows danced against the walls, pale threads of light floating through the window to fall against the silk of Miss Jen Pearl's dress. Bad memories needed to stay buried she thought as she rose from where she sat to pull her clothes from her body. Stepping into a cotton nightgown, Miss Jen Pearl lay back across the bed. Her mother continued to hum in the distance. A low murmur rose from Miss Jen Pearl's midsection as she followed the words seeping through the walls, Nana Leah reminding her that God was an on-time God and he would be there right on time.

FOURTEEN

On the sixteenth of October, Judge Hudson Jones dropped all charges against Graye. With apt precision Drake Tyler had shown cause for his client's dismissal, based on what he considered to be a blatant technical error on the part of the prosecution. The prosecution had argued every excuse they could muster and in the end the defense won, formalities and logistics winning out over what should have been just plain right versus wrong.

Ms. Jen Pearl could barely believe her ears when the good judge announced that Graye was to be set free. She watched in amazement as Drake and Graye shook hands like two old friends greeting each other for the first time, excitement wrapping arms around each other's shoulder. As she rose from where she sat she watched as Argie Steely rushed forward to get the first statement from the duo, then looked around in anguish as Tate Butler's family stormed out of the courtroom. The venom in Mrs. Butler's eyes confirmed what Miss Jen Pearl had feared most. Graye was coming home. The moment was surreal, their movements like a choreographed performance, danced with imperfection against a backdrop of silence. Miss Jen Pearl could feel her breath passing from her body.

Miss Jen Pearl sat back down against the wooden bench, her hands clasped neatly in her lap. She could feel her body begin to shake and she brushed the palms of her hands against the length of her thighs to still the quiver of muscle that would have dropped her to the floor were she to have stood back up. She forced herself to smile, a faint bending of her lips, as her son suddenly dropped his broad body down against the seat beside her, leaning his head against the round of her breasts as he pulled her hands to his lips, kissing the line of her fingers. Wrapping an arm around his shoulders, Miss Jen Pearl pulled him close as Drake grinned down at them. She shook her head, her eyes piercing his. She had warned him. Now there would be no turning back for any of them. Graye was coming home.

Angelette had always been able to feel Graye even before she saw him. His presence was like a dark secret hanging heavy in the air, invading space like nothing else could. Angelette could feel Graye even before she opened her eyes to find him staring down at her, a pained expression upon his face. His breathing was heavy, the rise and fall of his bare chest beating in unison with the heart beat that raced beneath his ebony skin. Graye stared down at her like she might disappear if he were to close his eyes too soon.

Angelette reached the length of her manicured fingers toward him, pressing Passion Pink nails into the granite of his stomach muscles. Graye flinched at the suddenness of her touch. Angelette smiled, the solid of Graye's flesh beneath her fingertips solidifying the fleeting imagery that had only moments before billowed through her dreams. She smiled again, leaning up to wrap her arms around Graye's body as he fell into her, the duo dropping back across the bed.

"My sweet, sweet baby," Graye whispered against her cheek, tangling his fingers through the strands of her hair. "I missed you, Baby Doll."

Angelette pulled him closer, losing herself beneath the weight of him. Their loving was quick. A rapid melding of flesh against flesh. Angelette was as hungry for him as he was for her and she clutched at him greedily, riding the tide of his loving with relative ease. Graye reclaimed what he thought to be his, marking his territory with the flow of warm semen that spilled from the length of his manhood. He fell atop Angelette with a heavy sigh, nuzzling the curve of her neck with his lips. He'd missed the sweetness of her, that edge of honey that coated his nerve-endings with her touch.

The warmth of the moment was suddenly chilled by the inflection of Angelette's words. "Why'd you try to kill me? Why Graye? Why'd you want to hurt me like that?"

Her naked body lay pressed against his, the curve of her buttocks leaning into the muscle against his upper thigh. Her upper body seemingly leaned away from him, the distance beginning to edge between them. Graye was familiar with the distance and it did not make him happy. He leaned over closer, groping her with a heavy hand, pulling at her in a futile attempt to close the sudden gap. Angelette continued to ask him questions, wanting only to know why he'd killed Tate Butler.

Graye sighed a deep mournful sigh as the echo of Angelette's voice filled the deep creases of his brow, danced a two-step across his heart, then settled down into the marrow of his bones. He hated when Angelette asked questions of him that he did not have the answers for. His lack of answers solidified his feelings of inadequacy and gave depth and dimension to emotions he thought would betray his manhood. With no answers or answers that made no sense, he felt himself to be less of a man.

Graye's feelings of weakness angered him. His being irate gave him back his control. Rage rose. Angelette could feel the heat of his anger rising against her back, the wealth of his temper burning in the fingertips that pressed heavily against the valley between her breasts. She braced herself for the fallout. Graye hovered above her, running his lips against the line of her ear, the edge of his teeth heavy against her flesh. When he answered, his voice was a low whisper, his breath hot against the side of her face. His answer came smooth and heavy, burning like acid against her skin. "It was the drink, Baby Doll. Jack Daniel's got the best a me. You know I love you. I wouldn't never do anything to hurt you. You know I didn't mean it."

Angelette fought the urge to push for more, her need to delve deeper into Graye's mind sinking like lead weight into the undersurface of her spirit. She wanted to relish the moment of Graye beside her, to remember the wealth of him that had once nurtured her well and made her feel whole. She needed to hang on to his words of love.

Turning to press herself against him, Angelette lifted her face into the curve under his chin, inhaling the scent of him. Graye pulled her closer, pressing his hands against her lower back, wanting to melt like snow beneath the warmth of her rays. She savored the taste of him against her tongue, relishing the zest of his salt and his sweet. Graye's rising rage withered with each pass of her tongue and morning found them still tangled in a bittersweet embrace.

FIFTEEN

They had neighbors who held hands when they walked. They were middle-aged, with four children between the ages of one and eight, and every day, right after dinner, rain or shine, they would stroll through the neighborhood holding hands. They seemed content with their ritual. It seemed to fit them as well as the brown tweed overcoat he wore on cool November days and the yellow rain slicker she wrapped around herself when the summer skies had opened overhead and spilled water down over Angelette's roses. It seemed to fit them well.

Sometimes Graye would watch them from the kitchen window as they came around the bend in the road, giggling quietly like high-schoolers, hand in hand. Other times he would toss up his hand or nod his head in greeting, waving hello from the refuge of the front porch as Angelette sat bent over her plastic flower beds. Graye would watch them, feeling like an intruder in some private moment of theirs, her fingers clasped firmly beneath his, the length of their strides perfectly executed. Graye could not remember the last time he and Angelette had held hands.

Graye watched from the kitchen window, just like he'd done every day since he'd returned home and when they were out of sight he went back to his searching. What was he hoping to find he wondered as he lifted her clothes from a bureau drawer to peek at the items she'd dropped beneath them. Not finding anything was what made him feel secure. It was the knowing that there was nothing there that gave him comfort.

As he poked through her papers, making note of each scribbled item, he thought about what the old woman had once said to him. "You best be careful Graye. You keep pokin' for nothin' and you might just find somethin' you don't want to find."

Nana Leah had been right. He knew it the moment he lifted the letter from its hiding spot and his comfort dropped to the floor beneath him. As he read the letter over and over again, it was as if the typewritten words were fuel for the venom that began to swell like brush fire within him. He was barely aware of the ball of crushed paper within his palm as he headed out the front door, racing to go find Angelette.

When you're seventeen-years-old love can bloom eternal. You can be enamored with the propensity of love and the potential for all love's greatness. You can be mesmerized by the warmth of a smile that says you are pretty enough and smart enough and more than enough woman to love the man that he is. Angelette had to have been mesmerized she thought as she watched Graye staring down at her. She had been mesmerized and now she found herself lost in the chasms of hurt that had followed.

The romance itself should have been the catalyst for her flight but Angelette had closed her eyes to the hurt, convinced that it could be better. She'd been convinced that Graye could be better because he had been by far the best. He had made her better because for the first time here was a man who said she was pretty enough and smart enough and more than enough woman to love the man that he was. When Angelette saw herself in Graye's eyes, she suddenly felt as if her value had increased, rising far above the pith of her crotch. What she saw in Graye's eyes did not peak at the border of her pubic hair.

But Angelette and Graye had fallen into a pretense that became the pattern for their existence. Their relationship revolved around Graye's wants and Graye's needs and even when she didn't agree, the pretense was better than the loneliness she'd known before Graye. It became the lifeline that kept them afloat and when Angelette stopped pretending, all hell broke loose.

Angelette heaved a heavy sigh, clutching the torn letter to her chest. Although her tears had already dried, she still sat cowering in the corner of the bedroom. The ink on the formal letterhead had bled into the ivory of the paper and she no longer recognized the words that had held so much promise for her weeks earlier. The gold embossed signet of Elon College's Admissions Department was all that remained legible.

From the moment they'd met it had been clear that Graye liked her, wanted to know her better, saw something within her that she had not yet learned to see in herself. There had been an edge to Graye's disposition, a wild spirit that intrigued Angelette. Despite the occasional hurt of it, that edge felt good to her. She welcomed it, nurtured it, learned from it, and in turn Graye loved her with complete abandonment. She became his and from that moment on he'd refused to let her go.

Graye paced a well-worn path into the carpeted floor, wringing the palms of his hands in exasperation. He'd screamed and yelled and had thrown things, breaking Angelette's possessions with little regard for their significance to her. As his insecurity raged down upon her, Angelette could feel herself no longer wanting to be his wife. She had no interest in retaining the title, wanting only to hand in her resignation from a job she'd grown to despise. With each passing day she only longed to walk out, not even bothering to say good-bye.

The feelings had been subtle at first, falling with the first tear, then building with each and every ugly word Graye spat in her direction. What seemed like an eternity had only been minutes until Angelette fell into the corner, her body defeated, her spirit bruised. And when all was done, when Graye finally fell onto his knees begging for forgiveness, Angelette felt her heart separate. That all-consuming hunger she'd once felt for Graye had been annulled, and she knew that there could be nothing more between them if she were meant to survive.

Graye wept, his tears dampening the front of his shirt. "Why? Why you want to leave me?"

Angelette shook her head. "I just wanted to go to school, Graye. I wasn't planning on going no where. I just wanted to go to school."

Graye's shoulders shook with each sob that racked the steel of his body. "Who did this for you? I know you didn't do this on your own. What man trying to take you away from me?"

Angelette pushed the shreds of paper into the pocket of her denim jeans. "No one, Graye. No one did this. I did it myself." The lie fell easily, the words numb against the woman's tongue. Angelette continued, her words controlled, her tone calming. "I just wanted to go to school to learn something for myself."

Graye stared at her past his tears, reaching out to stroke the side of her face where minutes earlier his palm had turned the flesh a brilliant shade of bruised red.

Angelette flinched at his touch, wanting to push his hands from her. "This ain't right, Graye. This ain't right. Why do you do this to me?"

Graye dropped his head into the palms of his hands, rocking back against his buttocks, his knees pulled into his chest. Angelette rose from where she sat, strode over to the bed and dropped down against the pillows.

There were no other words shared. Graye fell into the depths of darkness that he found most comfortable and Angelette allowed him to be. As night fell and darkness filled the small room, Angelette thought back to Tate and a whisper of words that had opened a door she would never have known existed.

Angelette did not know the man who stood cooling himself in front of the opened refrigerator. She stood watching him as he reached inside to pull a can of beer from the six-pack behind the apple juice and sliced baloney wrapped in wax paper.

Angelette stood watching him since he was blocking her path from the small bathroom to her freshly washed clothes laid out on the bed. She watched him until he finally noticed her presence and she instantly noted his sudden discomfort at her nakedness. The man was visibly embarrassed, his eyes darting from the floor to the ceiling and back again.

"Excuse me," he muttered, looking over his shoulders toward the door behind him.

Angelette blushed, crossing her arms in front of her. "I didn't know anyone was here. Graye ain't home and I was just finishing my bath."

Tate Butler absently fanned his hand. "No problem. Graye told me to just come on in. He didn't tell me anyone would be here."

Angelette nodded as she eased past Tate, reaching for one of Graye's button-downed shirts.

"My name's Tate. Tate Butler. Graye's my best friend." Tate smiled, finally allowing his eyes to rest upon Angelette's covered body.

Angelette smiled back, extending her hand toward Tate. "Nice to meet you. Graye done told me a lot about you."

Tate grinned. "He didn't tell me nothin' about you."

Angelette shrugged her shoulders, the smile upon her face widening. "Ain't much to tell. Graye's just been takin' care of me."

"You from around here?"

"Around."

Silence filled the air, wafting with the breeze that filled the room. Tate passed the beer can from one hand to the other, leaning to peer out the window for Graye.

"Graye says you go to school in Atlanta."

Tate nodded. "I'm a junior at Morehouse. I want to be a doctor."

Pulling at the freshly ironed shirt that encased her body, Angelette sat down on the pull-out sofa. "You must be really smart."

Tate shrugged. "I just study hard is all. Do you go to school?"

Angelette shook her head no, pulling a thumb into her mouth to bite at her nail. Her eyes darted back and forth across Tate's face, taking note of his fine features and the richness of his bronze complexion.

"You should think about going. I've been trying to convince Graye that he should go."

Angelette laughed. "I bet he don't like that."

Tate laughed with her. "You're right. He doesn't sit kindly for that at all." Tate paused, studying the young woman's face. "How old are you?"

"Nineteen," Angelette lied.

"You don't look nineteen. You barely look fifteen."

The girl's eyes dropped to her lap. "I'm nineteen", she mumbled, cutting her eye at Tate ever so quickly.

"You graduate from high school?"

Angelette shook her head.

"GED?"

The young woman continued to toss her head from side to side in response.

"Well, you should get your GED and think about college. I think you might like it."

"Really?"

Tate smiled. "Maybe if you go we can convince Graye to go."

The duo was interrupted as the front door opened and slammed closed.

"Go where?"

Tate jumped to his feet, spilling beer down the front of his denim jeans. "Hey man, what's up?" he said, brushing at the offending moisture with one hand as he gestured hello with the can of beer in his other.

Graye stared first at Tate, then shifted his gaze toward Angelette and back again. "What you two talking about?"

"We were just talking about school. I told Angelette she should think about going and that maybe we could get you to go too."

Angelette smiled a tentative smile. "Hey, Graye."

Graye nodded, not taking his eyes off Angelette. As she rose from her seat to come press a kiss against his cheek he noted the outline of her figure beneath the white fabric. The curvature of her frame was illuminated by the light shining through the window.

"So you met my woman?"

Tate nodded. "We were just getting acquainted. You just full a surprises ain't you, Graye. You could have warned me. I think I scared this girl to death just coming in like I do. I'll know to ring the bell next time."

"So, how long you staying?" Graye asked, wrapping his arm around Angelette's waist. The girl could feel his grip tightening as he pulled her close against him.

"Just here for the weekend for my daddy's birthday. My mama said to tell you she's cooking a big dinner tomorrow night and she expects to see you. I'm sure she'd love to meet Angelette, too."

"I'll let you know."

Tate nodded, feeling an uncomfortable tension starting to rise within the room. "You okay, Graye?" he asked, concern crossing his brow.

"Why wouldn't I be?"

"You seem upset."

"Do I have a reason to be upset?" He looked from Tate to Angelette and back to Tate.

Tate reached to place his half empty can into the kitchen sink. Striding over to his friend he extended his hand.

"Not here, brother. We ain't got no problem. I just wanted to come and tell you hello. Nothing more."

Graye stared at him momentarily, then reached out to shake his friend's hand. Angelette stood silently, observing the interaction between them.

"I'll be down at the bar later, I think. Maybe I'll catch up with you."

Graye nodded his head, adeptly chewing on a wooden toothpick. He didn't bother to respond.

"It was nice meeting you, Angelette."

The woman-child smiled, nodding her head as she brushed her hand against Graye's chest.

The door was barely closed tight behind the man before the back of Graye's hand slammed against the side of Angelette's face. Shock and pain broke her fall as the floor rose up to meet her.

Graye screamed. "Don't you ever have no other man in my house when I'm not home. You walking around half-dressed like you ain't got no damn sense. You must think I'm some kind a fool. You let him touch you?"

Angelette could taste the metallic tinge of blood against her tongue. "I didn't..." she started.

Graye pulled her to her feet, stilling the words that spun between then as he threw her against the bed. As he hovered above her, Angelette felt a wave of panic sweep over her, then just as quickly Graye dropped down beside her, tears rising to his eyes.

"I didn't mean to hurt you, baby. Lord, help me, what's wrong wit' me. I don't know why I did that. I don't know why. Please don't be mad at me, Angelette. Please don't be mad. You're my baby doll. You know I wouldn't hurt my baby doll." Graye's apology rushed past his lips, the wave of words spilling out of his mouth a mile a minute. Graye reached to kiss her forehead, her eyes, her cheek, her lips, wanting the heat of his kisses to dispel the cold that suddenly enveloped them.

Angelette heaved a heavy sigh at the memories. Tate had earned her that first slap. His presence had earned her many more over the years. But Tate had opened a door that Angelette hadn't been ready to see closed. In the darkness Graye still sat rocking to and fro.

Rising from the bed, Angelette reached a hand out to stroke the top of his head, leaning to kiss the man's forehead. "I'm going to your mama's, Graye."

"You still love me don't you, Angelette?"

The hollow of Angelette's words echoed about the room as she closed the door behind her. "Only you, Graye. Only you."

SIXTEEN

Miss Jen Pearl beat the palms of her hands against the rich, black soil of her flower beds. Anger ran down the length of her fingertips, spilling into the dark earth that housed the plastic stems she nurtured so warmly.

"I've told you time and time again, Graye. You can't beat a woman and expect her to want you."

"But I didn't hit her, Mama, I..."

The woman put a soil-stained hand up to still his lies. "You been tormenting that child since the day she arrived, and she has stayed and put up with you longer than you deserved. I don't care. Maybe you didn't put yo' hands on her this time, but you had no right to treat her the way you done. No right. I ain't raised you to be like that. Ain't nobody in this family ever been like that. Even yo' daddy, at his worse, treated a damn dog better than I've seen you treat Angelette." Miss Jen Pearl spat the words, her anger raging in Graye's direction. The man's head dropped heavily against his chest.

"You love me, Mama?"

Miss Jen Pearl closed her eyes, inhaling deeply, her mind racing to catch the words she thought her son needed to hear. Looking up at him, faint moisture pressed against her lashes. "Graye, you my son. I will always love you. But I'm not gone put up with your foolishness. I'm not. I took my share off yo' daddy. We had our bad times but we had more good times than anything. You stopped giving Angelette the good times and now you want to be mad 'cause she ain't happy."

"She want to leave me, Mama."

"No. She want to go to school. She want to have something that belongs to her. Something she earned, not something you gave to her or told her she could have. This is not about you, Graye. This is about Angelette."

"You don't understand, Mama. If she goes, Angelette ain't coming back."

"Then let her go, Graye. If that's what she wants, let her go."

Graye stared at his mother, the canvas of his expressions melting from pain, to sorrow, to emptiness. The light in his eyes was hollow and Miss

Jen Pearl could feel the darkness that lurked just beneath the surface of them.

"No," he said, his tone cold. "No. I didn't let Tate have her and ain't no one else gone have her either." Graye stormed back across the street, still screaming at her as he made his way home. "No one!"

The McAdams women were locked in heated debate as they sat at their mother's kitchen table. Nothing cooked on the stovetop, the pots and pans having been washed and put away for the evening. Miss Jen Pearl sat listening, too drained to offer any commentary to the conversation at hand.

"She a fool," Lake said, her head bobbing up and down. "Let a man hit me and see what happens."

"What you gone do?" Sister asked, staring intently at her sibling. "You ain't gone do nothing but stay. Just like Angelette."

Lake grunted. "Not me."

"Well, I might stay," Ginn interjected, "but he'd have to pay. He got to go to sleep sometime."

Lake laughed. "That's right. Make him find some religion. Be like Al Green."

"That's what I'm talking about," Ginn said, laughing with her. "Cook me up a pot a hot grits and help him find the Holy Ghost real fast."

Nana Leah rolled her eyes. "You girls is wrong to be talking like that. That poor child could a killed that man and what for? Ain't no man worth you losing yo' self over."

"Hmmph," Lake muttered under her breath.

"Why you think she stay?" Sister asked, looking from one McAdams' daughter to the other. "He done tried to kill her, done beat her, treat her bad and she still stay."

"She a damn fool," Lake answered.

Miss Jen Pearl cleared her throat. "She stays because she doesn't have any other choice.

Her daughters all turned to look at her. Miss Jen Pearl stared off into space. The room grew quiet as they waited for their mother to expand upon her statement.

Miss Jen Pearl turned her gaze toward her daughters. Her tone was low and quiet, a step above a whisper. When she spoke it was as if her words were rising from a hollow void, barely punctuating the air. "At first, she stayed because she was scared.

Angelette won't nothing but a baby when Graye bought her home. Ya'll know that. Came here running from something, thinking that Graye was going to make it all better. Then she stayed cause she loved him. Problem was she hadn't done enough living to really know what love was. Just knew that Graye wasn't as dark as what she'd been running from befo'. Thought that was love. After a while she just stayed cause this was all she knew. She knew what to expect. Knew what to do, when to do it, and if it got messed up, she knew how to fix it. Now," Miss Jen Pearl paused to take a deep breath, filling her lungs with air. Blowing the warm breath past her lips, her gaze met Nana Leah's before she continued. "Now, she stay cause she don't have any other choice. Graye done beat all of her choices out from under her and she think she ain't got none left."

"Well, someone need to tell her what to do cause she sho' nuff need to get as far from Graye as she can get," Lake said, nodding her head with finality.

Miss Jen Pearl rose from her seat. "He'll kill her dead first. It don't matter where she goes, Graye will find her and he will kill her dead before he will let her go."

"I'd still try if I was her," Lake said.

Miss Jen Pearl headed toward the door. She turned back around, staring from one face to the other. "She will," Miss Jen Pearl pronounced. "The day she decides she's already dead living with Graye like this, she will. She'll decide that her dead body can't be no worse than her dead spirit and she'll go. She may taste freedom for an hour, a day, or a year. But it won't matter, cause when Graye finds her, he will kill her dead."

Sister rose to wrap her arms around her mother's body. Miss Jen Pearl hugged her daughter back, holding onto the woman tightly, almost afraid to let go.

"What then, Mama?" Ginn asked. "What will happen then?"

Dropping her arms back to her sides, Miss Jen Pearl turned to look at Ginn, passing her gaze over her daughter's face, then she lifted her eyes to look at Lake. The muscles in her face seemed to twitch as if nervous, the quivering flesh her only answer as she turned and left the room.

Silence filled the cabinets and drawers, hovering over the drying dishes in the dish rack, occupying the empty space in the coffeepot and cups. Nana Leah answered the question. "Then nothing," the old woman said, her voice as low as Miss Jen Pearl's had been. "It'll be over then. We'll be burying the two of them together 'cause we'll lose Graye, too. We will lose our baby boy 'cause death will come to claim them both. You can mark my words. When it happens, death will come to claim them both."

Jen Pearl eased her body down the short length of hallway to her bedroom. Closing the room's door, she welcomed the comfort of silence that filled the space, the faint glow of a small nightlight radiating from the bedside. Her body felt heavy, decades of heartache suddenly weighing down upon her. As she dropped against the foot of her bed, she closed her eyes tightly, fighting to hold back her tears.

Dipping her head into her hands, Miss Jen Pearl pressed her fingers against the strained muscles that pulled tight across her forehead. Across the room, an oversized recliner seemed to beckon her to come sit, to settle herself against the worn brown-plaid cushions.

She and Otis had often sat together in that chair, her body curled comfortably against his as they watched the late night news on the small, black and white television set Otis had given her right after Graye had been born. That TV set still set on a table in the corner of the room. It had stopped working years ago but Miss Jen Pearl had never had any inclination to get rid of it.

As she sat with her memories, the reflections twisting and turning with her thoughts about her family, Miss Jen Pearl shivered, her body quivering in anguish. In her mind's eye, Otis shouted in her ear.

"Why do you need to be going to that center?" Otis demanded, tapping his foot against the wooden floor.

"The children like the community center, Otis. It gives them something to do after school when they're finished with their chores."

"And what you need to go for?"

"Do you not want me to go, Otis? Is that why you're yelling at me?"

The man shook a finger in her face, his words lost behind the anger that consumed him. He spun away from her, dropping into the newly purchased recliner that decorated the empty space in their large bedroom. The warm brown tones in the plaid fabric complemented the freshly painted taupe color that decorated the walls.

"I don't care what you do. You're going to do what you want to do anyway."

"Otis, I don't know what the problem is, or how to make it better if you won't explain it to me," she said softly.

"Ever since that doctor opened that center for them kids you been running down there like you get paid to be there."

"I just like to help out, Otis."

"I just bet you do. That damn doctor don't pay no bills in this house and he don't have no say in what you do."

Jen Pearl bristled as she studied her husband closely, his anger coating his words with bitterness. Jealousy hovered like a dark cloud over his head.

"I'm not gone argue with you about Doc Burton, Otis. Not again. I keep telling you that there is nothing going on with me and that man. That man has a wife and I have never done anything to disrespect you."

Pure hatred tripped across his face as she spoke the other man's name. "I'll kill you and him first, Jen Pearl. If I even think you stepping out on me, I will kill you. Got me a bullet with your name on it. So, don't think that I won't." The man pursed his lips, pushing them forward as he pushed and pulled at a wooden toothpick in his mouth.

She stared at her husband, studying the emotion stamped in the lines of his features. She couldn't understand the doubt and hostility that continually walked a tight line between them. She had always been a good wife, dutiful and obedient, putting Otis' needs well before her own. Even her children took a back seat to their father's long list of wants. His moods baffled her, the sudden shift in his temperament, running hot, then cold at the blink of an eye. She had no understanding of this man, knowing only that moments like this did nothing but disturb the tranquility of her home. She sucked in air, blowing it past her lips.

"I won't go to the center no more, Otis. If it will make you feel better. Just stop being angry about nothing," she said, her voice dropping to a low whisper. She lowered her body down beside his, prompting him to shift to make space for her on the recliner.

Otis wrapped his arms around her body, leaning to whisper against her ear, his breath blowing hotly against her flesh. "I mean it, Jen Pearl. I will kill you."

The woman shook her head from side to side. A rush of tears pressed against her eyes, saline burning against the back of her closed lids. "Hush now, Otis," she whispered. "You gone wake my babies with all of your foolishness."

Tilting her head upward, Jen Pearl pressed her lips to her husband's and kissed him. Hard. Otis allowed her mouth to skate over his, his lips pressed tightly together. Fueled by her urgency, he finally kissed her back, easing his tongue against hers. Giving into the moment, Jen Pearl savored the taste of him, allowing the stranger she loved so dearly to kiss the last trace of her hurt away.

Lifting her body from the seat, Miss Jen Pearl could feel the ghost of Otis billowing through the air. She waved it from around her, wanting to spin it and the memories out of the room. Stepping out of her clothes and into a flannel nightgown, she eased her full frame down against the bed, her thoughts running back to her youngest son, the child most like his father, and the woman who lived in fear at his side.

SEVENTEEN

Graye snored loudly, a fine line of drool puddling at the edges of his mouth, as he lay sleeping beside her. His breathing was tenuous as he sucked in air through his mouth and his nose. Angelette stared down at him, imagining what it would be like if he were to just stop breathing. Wondering how life would change if his heart just stopped pumping and blood no longer flowed through his veins. She imagined that time would simply stop, destiny racing to regroup as it reconfigured its rhythmn and got its cycle swinging again. She thought life would definitely manage to skip a beat if Graye McAdams were to just drop dead.

Rolling away from him, she curled up against the mountain of pillows behind her head. Graye barely moved as she turned her back to him, her gaze falling down the moonlit wall. How had she gotten to this place she thought. What had been the crime that put this sentence around her neck? Who had been the criminal?

Tate had told her once how God would punish generations for a sin committed by one. Angelette couldn't help but think that if her grandmothers had been anything like her mother, then perhaps she was still paying for all of their sins. She was thankful that she'd not had a daughter to pass the curse along to. Thankful that this affliction would one day end with her. Graye snorted, rolling to press his body against hers. His arm weaved around her waist, pulling her against him. She could feel his nakedness pressed against her flesh, the heat of his skin burning into hers. Angelette cringed at his touch, her heart broken when she remembered the times that she had yearned for Graye's touch. Her tears dripped silent against the pillow, her screams left deep inside her soul.

New Year's Eve had come and gone. Graye had taken her to the Easy-Slide Café for the festivities, ringing in the New Year with a bottle of Asti Spumanti and Funkadelic blasting from the sound system. She wore a new dress, one that Graye had picked out from Alexander's Department Store in town. The pale pink slip dress had fallen like silk against her skin. She'd felt grown, and beautiful, and Graye had beamed with pride, grinning like a Cheshire cat most of the night.

The party was still going strong when he grabbed her hand and pulled her away, the two of them walking slowly back toward his home.

"You have a good time?" Graye asked, the two of them holding hands and swinging their arms back and forth. "'Cause I had a good time."

Angelette smiled. "I did," she gushed, squeezing his fingers between her own.

They made the rest of the walk in silence until they reached the front yard. Seeing the lights still on in his mother's home, Graye had shouted loudly, screaming Happy New Years! at the top of his lungs. Angelette had laughed at his exuberance, waving to Miss Jen Pearl who had peeked past the curtains of her living room window.

Inside the small cottage, Graye stood nervous in the center of the room, eyeing Angelette with reservation. She smiled warmly, her gaze dancing over his features. She liked his eyes, the quiet coloration eerie and mysterious. She like that when Graye looked at her, it made her feel as if he saw something special. When Graye looked at her she always wanted to rush to the mirror to see what it was that he saw, to capture the image if only for a moment. She liked to see herself in Graye's eyes.

Graye smiled, nodding his appreciation. "I love you, Angelette," he said, his voice quivering slightly, nervous energy sweeping through his body. "I love you," he repeated.

They stood staring at each other, the clock on the wall ticking loudly, the faucet in the kitchen sink dripping steadily, and the hum of the refrigerator the only sounds bouncing between them. "Did you hear what I said, Angelette?" Graye asked whispering into the silence. "I love you."

Graye watched as Angelette took two steps toward him. She seemed to move in slow motion as she lifted her right hand to her left shoulder, pushing at the thin strap of fabric. She repeated the motion on the other side and the pale pink dress dropped to the floor around her ankles. Graye inhaled sharply as Angelette stood naked before him, stepping out of the tangle of fabric at her feet and making her way to stand directly in front of him.

Angelette reached for his hand, pulling his palm to her mouth. She pressed her lips gently against the brown palm, leaving a faint imprint of cherry-red lipstick against his skin. Graye stared at the image of her mouth against his hand as she lifted his fingers to her breast and wrapped his hand around the mouthful of flesh. She was warm, her temperature rising, and Graye couldn't help but think that if he held his hand there long enough one of them would be burned. Graye stepped in closer, kneading the tissue gently, his fingers grazing the protrusion of nipple that was as hard as rock candy. Rising to her toes, Angelette pressed her lips to Graye's, blowing warm breath past the line of his full lips. The kiss was gentle, and easy, and when she pressed her tongue along his, Graye could feel himself losing control. Her mouth danced against his mouth much like her body had danced earlier that evening. She did a slow grind against him, the movement of her lips slow and seductive, like a snake teasing its prey. Pulling away, Angelette looked up at him and smiled that smiled.

Lifting her into his arms, Graye dropped her against the bed. Angelette lay sprawled before him as the tension in his pants pulsed in tempo with his heartbeat. Tearing at his clothes, Graye tossed his shirt into the corner, leaving his pants and boxer briefs at the foot of the bed where he had stood.

Dropping down against her, he pulled both breasts to his mouth, lapping greedily at one and then the other. Crawling up the length of her body, he kissed a trail up along her neck, down the side of the face, brushing his lips against her eyelids as she watched him. Angelette opened herself to him, lifting her legs to wrap around his backside.

"You love me, don't you Angelette?" he asked, whispering into her ear, his words pleading. "You do love me, don't you?"

Staring up into his eyes, Angelette nodded her head and smiled. "Only you, Graye. Only you." With permission given, Graye poured himself into her, whispering her name again and again as he loved her, and Angelette hung on, refusing to let go.

"Why you crying?" Graye asked, his voice loud against her ear. Angelette ignored the question as Graye adjusted himself against her.

"Don't start, Angelette," he said, annoyance coating the inflection of his words. "You and this drama gone get on my nerves."

Angelette wiped at the moisture against her face. "I'm sad, Graye."

"What you got to be sad about?"

"The hurt don't never seem to stop, Graye. You and me and the fighting and I'm always feeling like I can't get it right and you always complaining that I'm getting it wrong. It just never seems to stop."

"So, this is my fault?"

"Forget it, Graye. I'm sorry. I didn't mean to wake you."

"No. You trying to leave me and you want to blame me for it. I didn't ask you to leave. I didn't tell you that you couldn't stay. You always got to be blaming me."

Graye was shouting, the tirade drowning out the wave of sobs that consumed Angelette. Rising above her, Graye pressed his hand over Angelette's mouth, his gaze piercing. "Don't," he admonished, easing the first quiver of an erection against the eve of her crotch. "I love you. Why can't you see it, Angelette?" he whispered into the pillow behind her head as he pushed his body into hers. "Why can't you see it?"

Angelette's breath caught deep in her chest as she struggled beneath the weight of him, his thoughts intent only on taking possession of her body. She closed her eyes, squeezing them tight in a concerted effort to rid her mind and heart of his presence. With a deep inhale and exhale of air, she reopened them to stare into space, no longer focused on Graye violating her body, her legs pushed rudely apart to bear the brunt of his sex beating the life from hers.

She didn't remember when it had become so easy to will her mind to that space over his shoulder, settling her spirit in the corner of the ceiling behind the webs of dust that clung to the paint. As Graye panted above her, his face contorted in rapture, Angelette counted in silence. She counted time, she counted lists of groceries, and errands, and things that had nothing to do with what was happening to her body sprawled open against the mattress. There was a line of demarcation that floated parallel to Graye, resting just above the curve of his buttocks and his broad back. Angelette imagined that Graye and the bare flesh and bones of her body lay together beneath this line. Everything else that was all her, watched from above, content with counting in the corner against the ceiling.

As Graye willed himself to linger longer, to extend his pleasure and her pain, Angelette struggled to remember when being with Graye had shifted into the valley of hell she now felt trapped in. She tried to focus on his face, wanting to understand the carnal pleasure painting his complexion. There was no beauty in the lines of lust that consumed him. Angelette could feel a swell of anger and bitterness rising within her, threatening to spew hatred from her eyes.

She detested her body's flagrant betrayal, her inner lining welcoming Graye inside, although her heart and head wished him away. It was the hollowest point of her shell that accepted him, the warm, moist cavity of her feminine spirit allowing him entry through her most private door. The betrayal was most profound because Graye believed this greeting to be something other than what it truly was. It was as painful as any one lie could be and the truth Graye read between the lines was anything but. Angelette closed her eyes tightly, gasping for air to fill her lungs. As she pushed the foul air past her lips, she willed her mind back to the corner and counted time, wishing for the ocean.

EIGHTEEN

The sun had risen early, then had disappeared behind a blanket of dark clouds, hiding from the rise of wind and rain that promised to pour down upon them. Graye stood in his front yard, staring toward his mother's house. Though there was no movement behind the sheer lace panels that curtained her windows, he knew that Miss Jen Pearl was up and awake, perhaps sitting with her first cup of coffee, or sorting through a pile of dirty clothes to start the laundry. No matter what it was that busied her hands, Graye knew that his mother was up and awake.

Pulling the brim of his baseball cap down low over his eyes, he headed up the street, cutting through yards and crossing lawns toward the old ball field behind the Men's Exchange Club. The freshly cut grass clung to his bright, white sneakers, the blue Nike emblem embedded on the side. Climbing the metal bleachers, Graye sat atop the steel seats, extending his legs before him. A rush of cool air hit him full in the face, the first drops of the day's showers beginning to rain down upon him. Graye lifted his face to the sky, relishing the cool wind and damp moisture that danced against his dark skin.

Tate had played football here. He had often looked up at Graye from the bench below imploring him to join them. Graye had always called the man a fool, ignoring his pleas. The other young men on the team had ignored Graye, silently grateful for his disinterest. But with each game, Tate would wave, wanting to share his excitement with his friend as the neighborhood league won game after game. Then Vanessa Bell and the private halftime show she'd given Gray had dispelled Tate's enthusiasm, running the man away from the game.

"You should play," Tate said, his eyes focused on the impending play and the offensive team navigating the visitor's end zone. "We could use a man like you on the team."

Graye shrugged. "I don't think so. I ain't got the time to waste."

"You here now, ain't you? What time you wasting?"

Graye changed the subject. "You going to the club after?"

Tate shook his head, his gaze still focused on the field as his teammates pushed their way to a touchdown. He jumped up excitedly, giving a loud cheer before he returned to his conversation with Graye. "Nah. Got me a date. Taking Vanessa Bell to the movies."

Graye cut his eye at his friend. "Since when you start seeing Vanessa?"

Tate grinned, meeting Graye's gaze with his own. "We been dating for a while now. She sweet, ain't she?"

Before Graye could answer, the coach signaled for the defense and Tate rushed out onto the field. Spotting Vanessa sitting with a group of girls at the other end of the bleachers, Graye eased his way over to her side, a sly grin gracing his face.

"Hey, girl. What's up?" he said, standing at her elbow, his eyes focused on Tate playing out on the field.

Cutting her eye from one friend to the other, Vanessa smiled sweetly. "Not much. How you doing, Graye?"

"Better now, girl. Your pretty smile done brightened up my day."

As Vanessa rolled her large black eyes, the other young women giggled beside her. "You still in school?" Graye asked.

"You know I graduated last year, Graye. I was a year behind you and Tate. I work over at the Dollar Store now. I'm an assistant manager and I go to school at night. I'm studying to be a nurse."

"I hear you sweet on my boy Tate."

"He tell you that?"

"He done told me a lot a things about you, girl."

"Like what?

Graye shrugged, ignoring her question. She asked again. "What Tate done told you about me, Graye McAdams?"

When Graye smiled, his eyes washing over the lines of her lean body, the girl felt herself blush, a rush of color rising to her café au lait cheeks. She flipped her newly pressed bob from side to side, the long strands of black hair waving against her face. "I know he didn't tell you that," she said indignantly, her tone changing.

"Tell me what?" Graye said sheepishly, still grinning. "I see where you're mind is at. You know Tate wouldn't never say nothing bad about his girl."

Vanessa blushed. "He say I'm his girl?"

Graye shrugged. "Maybe."

"Boy, you like to play too much," Vanessa said, waving a hand toward Graye. Catching her fingers in his own, Graye gently stroked the length of her palm. The warmth of his touch was teasing and Vanessa drew her hand back, pressing it between her thighs. Graye laughed, nodding his head slowly. His gaze left her face and spanned the length of the field looking for Tate. He stood silent as he watched the man huddled in tight formation with his team. Turning to stare back at Vanessa he smiled again, his eyes conversing with hers. When he gestured toward the parking lot, the movement ever so slight, and brushed his fingertips against the side of her leg, he knew she would follow. He knew curiosity alone would draw her to him and his lying tongue would hold her close.

Some thirty minutes later, as the crowd scattered, Tate looked around for his friend and his new girl. Vanessa's friends had only shrugged when he'd asked about her, rushing off in hushed whispers as they swept past him. He'd watched as they pushed their way past Graye's car, a white Ford Thunderbird with fire-engine red leather seats. Vanessa's friend Gayle knocked hurriedly on the tinted window, casting a glance over her shoulder in his direction when she did. When Vanessa lifted herself from the car, pulling at her clothes, Tate could feel his heart drop deep into the pit of his stomach. Graye eased out behind her, leaning brashly against the front of the vehicle. As Graye pressed Vanessa's silk panties to his nose, Tate's heart burst, spewing venom into his bloodstream.

Understanding filled the two hundred feet of distance between them. As the two men locked eyes, silence clouded the air, replacing the wealth of chatter that had surrounded them minutes before. Even the birds had ceased their singing. As Tate struggled to will his limbs to move, to pull himself from the pit of heartbreak he'd fallen into, Graye slid into the driver's seat of his automobile, dropping Vanessa's undergarment to the ground as he pulled out of the space and headed down the road.

Graye ignored the swell of rain that washed over him, his clothes thoroughly drenched. He dropped a packet of saturated cigarettes under the bleachers. Tate had eventually forgiven him that indiscretion, just as he'd forgiven all the others. Tate always did, believing Graye would learn from his example. Graye had stored that lesson with all the others, slivers of memories filed somewhere in his head.

Everything Tate had ever had, he'd given to Graye, sharing his wealth freely. Graye had not been so generous. But when Tate had taken Angelette's love, its possession was more than Graye could have ever imagined. It ravaged the already fragile bonds of their friendship, lessons of forgiveness escaping Graye completely. Easing his body off the bleachers, Graye headed back towards home, the torrent of rain a mere shadow beneath his tears.

Miss Jen Pearl met her son at the door. She eyed him slowly, her gaze sweeping from the top of his head, down to the feet planted firmly on the floor mat outside her back door. Graye was soaked through, his clothes dripping wet with moisture. He seemed smaller standing there, his massive six foot, six inch stature appearing to have shrunken and withered beneath the cold. Shaking her head, she gestured for him to stay where he was, and Graye did, understanding sweeping between their two gazes.

Miss Jen Pearl took no time at all to retrieve two large towels and by the time she'd returned to his side, Graye had stripped down to his briefs, tossing his clothes into the dryer on the back porch. He sat on an old wooden bench that decorated the small expanse of screened porch, his large body occupying every square inch of the padded seat.

"You gone catch pneumonia out in this weather," Miss Jen Pearl said softly, swiping at her son's head with the plush cloth and drying the wetness from his face. She paused to lift his chin with the palm of her hand, his gaze meeting hers. She stared at him for a quick minute, wanting to say something but not knowing the words. Her thoughts played like an old tune in her mind, the familiar melody lost only because she was trying to remember. Instead she leaned down to press her lips to his cheek and gestured for him to follow her inside.

"Why you out in this weather, baby?"

Graye shrugged. "Just walking."

"You want something to eat?

Shaking his head from side to side, Graye dropped down onto a padded chair, pulling one of the towels onto his lap and the other over his shoulders. "Could use a cup of hot coffee though."

His mother said nothing as she reached for an empty mug out of the kitchen cabinet and filled it from the percolator that sat on top of the stove. After topping it off with three spoonfuls of sugar and a dash of cream, she placed the cup of hot fluid on the table top before him. After making one for herself, her third that morning, she dropped into the seat across from her son and took a slow sip.

The television was playing in the other room, Bob Barker's voice ringing into the open air, followed by a roar of applause for some contestant who'd managed to win a brand new refrigerator. The duo sat listening, though neither was really paying any attention to *The Price Is Right* or the rash of commercials that aired every few minutes. Graye sat staring into his cup, his hands clasped in his lap. Every so often he'd lean forward, dropping his lips to the brim as he slurped up fluid into his mouth. Miss Jen Pearl would lift her own cup to her lips, savoring the rich fluid as it filled her mouth and slid with ease down her throat.

Graye finally broke the silence that hovered awkwardly between them. "I didn't mean to kill Tate, Mama. I didn't," he said matter-of-factly. "I know you think I done it on purpose, but I swear I didn't."

Miss Jen Pearl eased her cup back to the tabletop as she met his stare with one of her own. Graye continued.

"You know Tate was my best friend. I didn't mean to hurt my friend like that. Didn't mean for it to happen at all," he said nonchalantly.

The woman waved her head slowly. "But you did kill him, Graye, whether you meant to or not. You did it. You was wrong, Graye. Tate ain't deserve you doing that to him. Tate loved you. That boy would have done anything for you and you know it. You ain't had no business even thinking about pointing no gun at Tate. And what about what you done to Angelette? Would it have been on purpose if you'd had some bullets left when you pointed that gun at her and pulled the trigger?"

Graye hung his head, his mother's gaze still piercing through him like the sharp edge of a dagger. When he looked back up, she was still shaking her head. Graye shrugged as he leaned back into his cup, his hands still locked in his lap. He sucked up a mouthful of fluid, rinsed it around in his mouth and swallowed it hard. As he sat upright, pulling himself up taller in his seat, he met his mother's gaze one more time.

His words fell slowly, his tone harsher than it had been just seconds before. It was a shade of Graye his mother knew all to well, that side of her son most folks avoided or ran from. "You know they was wrong, Mama. You know it just like I do. They was wrong. I told them both what could happen, but they didn't listen. So I had to do what any man would have done if' he had to." Graye's head swung harshly from side to side, every muscle in his body clenched as if in preparation for a fight. "It didn't have to happen like it done. Tate could of made sure things was right between us, but he didn't. I'm sorry he dead 'cause I sure 'nuff didn't mean to kill him, but it sure could have been different if Tate had just left my woman alone."

The woman paused only briefly before responding, her head still waving from side to side against her thin neck. "Why does that sound like you done it on purpose, Graye?" she asked, the chill to her own tone edged in barbs of ice. Graye said nothing, his eyes narrowing into thin slits before he leaned back down to drink from his cup. Having nothing else to say Miss Jen Pearl heaved a deep sigh as she pulled herself onto her feet. She barely bothered to toss one last look in her son's direction as she made her way out of the room, moving back to the television set as the beginning of *Young and the Restless* played on the screen. Before she had settled herself comfortably on the sofa, Graye had followed behind her, those towels wrapped modestly around his body. He dropped down to the seat beside her, leaning to rest his head against her lap.

"You love me, Mama?" he asked softly, his voice barely audible over the volume of the television set.

Miss Jen Pearl brushed her fingers down the side of his face, gently caressing the soft skin that curved around his cheek and brushing at the tight wisps of curls that edged his hairline.

"You do, don't you?" he asked again, his voice pleading.

His mother nodded her head as she blinked back the moisture that clouded her vision. "Of course I do, Graye" she answered, one tear brushing against her thick lashes. "Of course I do."

"Of course I do," Miss Jen Pearl was saying to her mother, the older woman staring at her intently. "He's my child. How can I not love him?"

"Then you needs to do something to get him some help," Nana Leah concluded. "Somethin' ain't right with that boy."

"He's a man now, Mama. Not a boy. I can't make choices for Graye no more. He's got to make them for himself."

The matriarch shook her head. "Mark my words, Jen Pearl. That boy gone hurt someone or himself some day. Look at him out there, acting a fool. Don't make no kind of sense," she said as she moved herself away from the front window and back into an oversized arm chair. "No kind of sense at all."

Jen Pearl moved to where her mother had been standing, easing the curtain out of her view as she peered into the front yard. Graye and his best friend Tate stood toe to toe. It was obvious the conversation was more argument than anything else, the young men posturing like two pitbulls squaring off for a fight. She shook her head as she took a deep inhale of breath, filling her lungs with oxygen.

Moving through the front door, she made her way to the top of the porch steps, still staring at the duo who were both shouting obscenities at each other. Before she could comment Graye swung, his arm rotating from its socket as his clenched fist connected with Tate's jaw. Jen Pearl felt the solid punch that swung the boy's head back against his shoulder. Then Tate swung back, his own fist slamming squarely into Graye's chest, knocking the breath from his lungs. Before she could blink the two were rolling across her front year, anger clutching one to the other as they flailed back and forth against each other.

Jen Pearl heard herself scream, calling out her son's name, her own anger rising steadily. "Graye McAdams! You and Tate stop that mess, right now! You hear me? I said stop it!" Without realizing it she'd snapped a fresh branch from the large oak that shaded the front yard and was swinging it back and forth. It lashed skin, striking Graye and Tate on bare arms and broad backs.

Graye lifted his hands up in defense. "Stop, Mama! I ain't do nothing!"

"You out here acting like you ain't got no good sense. You and Tate both. You two want to act like children, I'm gonna tear up both your behinds."

Both young men sat back on their buttocks as Miss Jen Pearl stood over them, both her hands resting against her wide hips, the switch still clutched in the palm of her hand.

Tate swiped at the perspiration that was dripping into his eyes. "Sorry, Mrs. McAdams but Graye started it."

"And I'm gone finish it too," Graye said, his tone threatening.

Miss Jen Pearl lifted the switch over her head. "I said it's finished now. Just 'cause you think you too grown to get whupped don't mean I won't still do it."

Graye rolled his eyes, his gaze dropping to the ground as he pressed his chin into his chest.

"What you two out here fighting about?" she asked, looking from one to the other.

Both shrugged, snatching a glance toward the other. Neither responded.

"You two out here trying to kill each other and neither one of you knows why?"

"It was stupid, Mrs. McAdams. Just something stupid."

Miss Jen Pearl glanced down at the watch on her thick wrist. "Graye, you gone be late for work. Go on inside and get yourself cleaned up before you're late."

Her son lifted himself onto his feet. He paused for a quick minute, then reached a hand toward Tate. He braced himself as Tate took it, allowing Graye to pull him up onto his own feet. Without saying anything he pushed past his mother and headed inside the family home.

Tate rubbed his fingers against his bruised jawbone. Opening and closing his mouth he shook his head, testing to see if anything might actually be broke.

Miss Jen Pearl heaved a deep sigh.

Tate apologized once again. "I'm sorry, Mrs. McAdams. I just..."

"I know, child," she said cutting him off. "I know you can't let Graye run all over you. You let him do it to you once and he'll just keep doing it. I know you got to stand up to him sometimes."

Tate nodded. "It'll be okay. He'll cool down in a few days and things will be like normal between us."

Dropping the switch to the ground below, Miss Jen Pearl reached her arms out to give Tate hug. She kissed his cheek, then pushed him toward the other direction. "Go on home, baby. Tell your mama I said hello."

"Yes, ma'am. I will."

As she watched him leave, Jen Pearl marveled at the depth of friendship that kept Tate in her child's life, the young man coming back each and every time Graye pushed him away. *Almost like he got himself his own guardian angel*," she mused, deep in thought as she thought about Graye and all his ills. Tate had surely been a God send, she thought, his influence keeping Graye on the straight and narrow as much as was humanly possible. Anyone else would have left Graye alone ages ago.

Turning an about face she met her mother's gaze the woman staring at her from the living room window. Nana Leah shook her head, her expression saying again what Jen Pearl already knew.

NINETEEN

Plastic flowers die. When their stems and leaves wither under the summer heat, they seem no different from their organic cousins. The newness and vibrancy of real and fake disappears into the same realm of ugliness. Color wanes pale and there is no potential for new growth readily evident.

Miss Jen Pearl pulled weeds and plastic petals simultaneously, tossing both into an oversized trash bag at her side. Gardening gloves covered her aging hands, protection against the dark soil that she played in. Angelette was kneeling before the other flowerbed, imitating her mother-in-law, enjoying the quiet and the warmth of sunshine beating against her shoulders. Having no gloves, dirt caked her fingers, packed tightly beneath the short length of her nails. Angelette enjoyed the feel of the rich earth against her hands and she played like a child would play, pretend cakes and cookies molded neatly against the lawn.

Miss Jen Pearl turned to watch her, staring intently at the woman who was still more child than adult. "You getting anything done over there?" she asked, nodding in Angelette's direction.

The woman giggled. "I am. I was just remembering how I use to have tea parties in the mud when I was little."

Miss Jen Pearl smiled, her head still bobbing up and down. "So", she said, shifting her body to sit on the lower porch step, "When do you start school?"

The smile on Angelette's face disappeared, fading so quickly that if one had not seen it, they would never have known it had been there in the first place. Her gaze raced from the older woman's face, down to the ground, then out into the distance beyond the boundaries of the front yard. She fell back against her buttocks, settling herself against the lush green grass.

"You still going, aren't you?" the older woman prodded.

The two women studied each other, one stare as intense as the other, before Angelette heard herself responding. "I'm not going. Not this year. Maybe some other time."

Miss Jen Pearl shook her head, slowly moving it from side to side. She noted the rise of tears that pressed at Angelette's eyes, the quiver of the young woman's bottom lip, and the tight band of muscle clenched along her jaw line.

"What you want to do with your life, Angelette? What do you dream about, Baby Doll?"

Angelette shrugged.

Miss Jen Pearl pressed on. "You must have some dream for yourself, Angelette?"

The young woman pondered the question, time ticking slowly as she searched herself for an answer. She cut her eyes in Miss Jen Pearl's direction, then turned her gaze back out into the open air. Miss Jen Pearl could almost see the wheels of deliberation spinning in the girl's head, thoughts and memories tumbling about and shifting for space as she moved her mind to other times and other places. When she finally thought to answer, the sun had actually shifted its place in the sky, settling just a little lower against the horizon. "One day I'd like to see the ocean," Angelette finally whispered. "I've never walked barefoot in sand before."

Miss Jen Pearl stared at her, unable to make sense of her response. The confusion graced her face and prompted Angelette to continue.

"My mama once told me that when you stand at the edge of the ocean, at that spot where the water kisses the sand, something happens to you, something special. She said it makes you feel like a bird might when it can get itself out of a cage. It was the only thing I remember her telling me that was ever worth remembering." Angelette's gaze was still locked with her mother-in-law's as the woman slowly nodded her understanding. The exchange of silence that swelled in thick waves between them spoke volumes.

She'd had her own dreams once. Before her marriage they had not included nine children or a man who had been as hateful as Otis McAdams had sometimes been. After her children had been born, her dreams had revolved around each of them, hopeful introspections of what she hoped for their lives and hers. The few times she'd been moved to complain or whine about her existence, Nana Leah had saw fit to tell her that her lot in life could have been worse. Much worse. And, she needed to be grateful that God allowed her to get up each morning and lay back down each night. The black and white of it had seemed easy for Nana Leah, but Jen Pearl had been desperate for just a hint of pigment to color her way.

As Miss Jen Pearl sat behind the closed door of her bedroom, perched anxiously on the edge of the bed, she couldn't help but be upset that she couldn't for the life of her, remember what those dreams had been. Years before they'd been vivid entries in every aspect of her life, the details playing against the backdrop of her mind like a full-length movie. She had shared them only once with Otis and his response had brought her to tears, moving her to shift her fantasies as far from his reach as she could muster.

"What you daydreamin' 'bout now?" the man had asked, eyeing her with annoyance as she stood on the front porch, a new baby cradled in her arms while the rest of her brood toddled about in the dusty front yard. She had been staring off into space for a few good minutes, oblivious to the noise that rang across the yard.

Jen Pearl had shrugged her shoulders. "Was just thinking about what it might be like to live in one of them big houses over by Harvey Walker's farm. Them some pretty new houses, don't 'cha think?"

The man had scoffed as he dropped his body down against an old kitchen chair that sat on the corner of the porch. A toothpick protruded from the corner of his mouth, the wooden appendage dancing back and forth across the fullness of his bottom lip. Jen Pearl smiled in his direction, shifting her new baby against her breast.

"If we lived in one of them houses I bet we'd have enough room to give all these kids they own rooms and still have space left over. I'd have a bigger garden and we could plant vegetables and flowers. You could have you a garage to work on that new truck in and build that pretty furniture that you like to make. We could have us some big parties on all that land, I bet 'cha!" Jen Pearl exclaimed, a wistful expression adorning her youthful face as she fathomed the possibilities.

Otis had grunted his disinterest.

"I had me a dream the other night, Otis, that our babies was all grown up and me and you was traveling around the world to all kinds of new places. I sure would like for us to do that one day, wouldn't you? Wouldn't that be something, Otis?"

Otis shook his head, spitting a wad of vile phlegm over the porch rail. Jen Pearl watched as it landed on the leaves of the rose bush that sat at the end of the porch. The spittle clung to one of the new buds, spoiling the beauty of the red bloom with its ugliness. She frowned, disgust filling her eyes.

"You a fool, woman. You a God-damn fool. Your problem is you dream to much, always wanting what you ain't never gone have."

Jen Pearl bristled slightly, careful not to disturb the sleeping infant. "Why you have to be so mean to me, Otis? Ain't nothing wrong with having a dream to hold on to."

"You dream too big, wanting to hold on to stuff I can't give you. Trying to make me feel bad 'cause I ain't no big time doctor like that white man."

Jen Pearl shook her head, heaving a deep sigh of exasperation. "I don't know what that man has to do with me having myself a dream. My daddy use to say if you reach for the moon you bound to catch you a star or two on the way up. My dreams is my moon and they supposed to be big."

Otis came to his feet, moving to the top step as he looked out over the land, barely taking note of the children that were his, playing happily in the distance. He laughed, the sound of it harsh. Stepping down off the porch, he paused at the bottom step, turning to look up at her.

"You still a damn fool. I don't know why I waste my time with your sorry ass. Dream all you want, fool. 'Cause you and I both know ain't a one of them ever coming true. You was nothing when I married you and you nothing now. Won't be nothing, won't have nothing."

A rush of warm saline filled her eyes. Her bottom lip quivered ever so slightly as Otis headed in the direction of his truck.

"Where you going, Otis?" she asked softly, her tone reflecting the hurt he'd slapped her with.

"Down to the club. Had me a dream I was gone find me a real woman worth my time there," he said, the bitterness of his laughter following his words. "Hopes my dreams come true, too," he concluded as he eased his way into the vehicle, started the engine and pulled out of sight.

Miss Jen Pearl heaved a deep sigh as she lifted herself from the bedside. There were chores to finish and dinner to fix before she would be through for the day. The work that sat in wait of her seemed to be calling for her attention as she sat absorbed in thoughts and accosted by memories that served no useful purpose.

Perhaps she had been a fool she thought, the notion briefly filling her mind. Staying with Otis had probably been the most foolish thing she had done. Otis hadn't deserved the love she'd crowned him with, declaring him king of her provence the moment they'd met. Otis had surely not deserved her. The memories rode her spirit, saddling up beside her musings about Angelette and Graye. Miss Jen Pearl knew that time had passed her by, gone far too long for there to be any change, but perhaps, she suddenly pondered, things could be different for Angelette. Perhaps, if Miss Jen Pearl could have her way, Angelette could learn to dream. From somewhere off in the distance she could hear her mother calling out her name. Miss Jen Pearl heaved a deep sigh. There were too many things to be done and no one to do it but her.

Nana Leah sat on the bedside, old age holding her hostage against the mattress. Her limbs ached and the pain that throbbed a steady beat in her joints was keeping her tied to her room. She inched her buttocks closer to the edge of the mattress, pressing her swollen feet against the carpeted floor. She rocked her calloused soles back and forth across the surface of the well-worn shag threads, tickling the stubby length of her toes. The woman struggled to pull herself up, willing her short legs to hold her tall and not send her falling to the floor. She was weaving from side to side, trying to steady her balance when Miss Jen Pearl poked her head into the room.

Making her way to her mother's side, Miss Jen Pearl offered the old woman an arm to brace her body against. "Where's your walker?" she asked, her tone scolding, her eyebrows raised.

"Don't need no walker."

Miss Jen Pearl shook her head. "You need it to balance with when you get up, Mama. You can use your cane after that."

"Don't need no cane," Nana Leah responded. She eased a floral printed housecoat over her shoulders as her daughter held the garment open for her.

The younger woman rolled her eyes, changing the subject. "Are you hungry?" Do you want something to eat?"

Nana Leah shook her head. "No, thank you. Had me some apple juice and it went sour on my stomach. I don't feel so good. I got gas and it's cramping my stomach."

"You should eat something."

The older woman rolled her eyes. "You had a telephone call. That white man called for you."

Miss Jen Pearl ignored her mother's nasty tone, the ugly she'd steeped her words in, bitter and pungent. Whenever the woman spoke of Doc Burton, her tone was acrid, filling the air with a dark malignancy. She pulled the sheets and covers neatly over the two pillows at the head of the bed.

"You hear me?" Nana Leah said, taking a seat in the reclining lift chair that sat in the corner of the room. "I said, that white man called looking for you," the woman repeated, spitting venom with each word.

Miss Jen Pearl refused to look in her mother's direction, feigning interest in sorting a pile of her mother's laundry.

Nana Leah grunted. "Don't know what he keep calling you for. He ain't got no reason to be calling here."

Miss Jen Pearl bristled, heaving a loud sigh. "Doc Burton is a friend, Mama. He calls because he cares about how we're all doing."

Nana Leah chuckled, shaking her head from side to side. "Jen Pearl, that man been sniffing behind you since forever. With all the trouble he done caused you, you shouldn't want him to be calling you for nothing."

Miss Jen Pearl rolled her eyes, pursing her lips with distaste. She rolled her tongue inside her cheek, her mother's attitude leaving a rancid film inside her mouth. She bit down against the appendage. Biting to keep from responding with rank discord. Biting back words of raw sewage that threatened to spill out into the room.

Nana Leah grunted again, turning her attention to the remote in her hand, pushing at the buttons to lift her legs. She settled herself comfortably against the pillows behind her head. Still muttering under her breath, words fell a mile a minute, the low drone disturbing the room's quiet. "Trouble always sitting right in front of you, Jen Pearl, and you can't see it. I point it out to you and you still refuse to see it."

"Mama, I ain't in the mood for this today. I'm tired and I don't want to hear no nonsense from you."

Nana Leah sucked her teeth. "Trouble right at your door, knocking to get in. Done told you before. Told you about that white man causing you all that trouble with Otis."

"Otis is dead, Mama."

Nana Leah ignored her. "White man caused all that trouble and he still sniffing after you. Didn't learn nothing. You see what happened with that nice boy, Tate. Told you before about him being nothing but trouble for Angelette. Bless her heart. Now he dead and your boy who done it half crazy over it. Nothing but trouble, just like I told you."

"Yes, Mama." Miss Jen Pearl picked up a load of dirty clothes from the floor. "I've got to do the laundry, Mama. Call me when you ready for your food."

Nana Leah continued to mutter under her breath. "Nothing but trouble. Don't know why you don't see it. Trouble like dog mess waiting for you to step into it. Smell stank, look stank, and you tiptoeing all around it, stead of getting it up out of your way."

Miss Jen Pearl rolled her eyes, not bothering to comment as she made her way out of the room. Nana Leah's dissertations had become common place, perception-based rhetoric asserted as definitive fact. Miss Jen Pearl had lost count of the number of times her mother had deemed it necessary to proclaim her knowledge of trouble, pointing a finger in Jen Pearl's direction as an "I told you so" flooded the old woman's face.

Dropping the pile of soiled panties, white socks and cotton tee shirts to the floor in front of the washing machine, she leaned her body against the appliance, allowing it to support the sudden flood of weight that consumed her.

She and Doc Burton had only known each other a few months the first time Nana Leah had called him trouble, pasting the label against his chest like a nametag. She had called him trouble, defined him as problematic, viewing the man as a foul addiction Jen Pearl needed to be saved from. When Otis' jealous outbursts had served to validate the old woman's appraisals, authenticating her pronouncements, Nana Leah had shaken her index finger, "I told you so" becoming her daily mantra.

The two women stood in the rear yard, clipping a freshly washed load of clothes to a length of clothesline that ran from the corner of the house to the large oak tree that bordered the edge of the property. Overhead, the afternoon sun played hide and seek in a cloud filled sky, skipping in and out of the billowy vapors with ease. The temperature had swelled to record levels, the summer air hot and humid. Jen Pearl swiped at the moisture that dampened her brow. Her mother chided her to hurry so they could get finished. Her baby girl, July, slept peacefully in the basket between their feet while her other children ran in circles from one end of the yard to the other. Both women looked up as the black sedan pulled into the yard, dust floating into the air from beneath the turning tires. Nana Leah gave her only child a quick glance, annoyance painting her expression.

"What that man want now?" she asked, her hands falling to her spreading hips. "Ain't no one here sick."

Jen Pearl shrugged, not bothering to respond as she made her way toward the tall, white man who'd lifted his lean body from the vehicle.

"Doctor Burton, what brings you out here this afternoon?" Jen Pearl smiled sweetly, the even row of her white teeth filling the beauty of her face.

The man smiled, his deep, blue eyes shining brightly. "Good afternoon, Jen Pearl. I was in the neighborhood so I thought I'd just check to see how you were doing."

"That was sweet of you. We're all just fine, thank you."

"How's that baby?"

Jen Pearl smiled, gesturing toward her mother who'd reached to pick the child up into her arms. "She's just fine. Growing fast."

Horace Burton nodded, waving his hand in Nana Leah's direction. "Good afternoon, Mrs. Mosley."

The woman waved her hand, eyeing him curiously. "Afternoon, Doctor. How's Mrs. Burton doin'?"

"She's just fine. Thank you for asking."

"Tell her I said hello."

"I'll do that."

Nana Leah continued to stare in his direction, rocking the baby against her shoulder.

The doctor turned his attention back to the woman beside him. "And you're feeling better, Jen Pearl?"

"I am. I'm doing just fine. Don't know what we would have done without you, Doctor Burton."

Still smiling, the man stood awkwardly, his body swaying in the summer heat. High humidity was dancing under the summer rays, and the air was full and hot and desperate for relief, much like Doctor Burton's body suddenly felt. His gaze glided across the yard to the children playing in the sand, and the old woman who was still staring harshly, back to Jen Pearl's dark, wide eyes and full lips. He felt himself gasp ever so slightly as she smiled, the warmth of it flooding her face. His muscles suddenly quivered with excitement and heat rained South as the front of his crotch suddenly pulled tight against his slacks. He lifted the black medical bag he'd been holding to the front of himself.

"Well, I need to be going. I'll stop by again to check on you and your children, Jen Pearl. Just to make sure everyone's doing well," he added.

Jen Pearl smiled, her gaze meeting his. She felt herself swimming in the blue of his eyes, a blue so deep it made her think of large pools of cool water. His gaze was caressing, blowing sweetly from her head to her bare feet and back again. His stare sent shimmers across her spine and her breasts suddenly swelled full, baby's milk seeping from the rock hard nipples. She ignored the two circles of dampness that pressed against the front of her sundress.

"You have a good afternoon, Doctor Burton. Tell Mrs. Burton we was asking about her."

The man nodded as he sat back in his car, waving his hand as he pulled the vehicle out of the yard. Nana Leah came to her side as Jen Pearl stood watching him as he drove off down the road. Passing the baby girl to her mother, the woman clucked loudly, her head waving from side to side.

"You better watch that man, Jen Pearl. He ain't nothing but trouble and you don't need no trouble between you and Otis."

Jen Pearl sighed. "Mama, you don't know what you talking about. I need to go feed this baby."

Nana Leah continued to nod. "Don't mess up, Jen Pearl. Here me when I tell you. You don't need that kind of trouble and that man was eyeing you like you was his favorite piece of candy. Won't no good come of him showing up here any time he please. No good." The woman's head bobbed up and down against her shoulders as she continued. "You're married to a good man, Jen Pearl. He take good care of you and these here children. Don't you mess that up," Nana Leah professed.

"Yes, ma'am," Jen Pearl answered, her own daughter suckling at her breast and her gaze still lost in the waft of dust lifted to the air by the turn of the white man's tires.

As the memory swept past her, Miss Jen Pearl thought about her mother, wondering if Nana Leah had ever thought about a man the way she had sometimes thought about Doc Burton. Her days of fantasy were long gone, but she remembered a time when just the sheer thought of the man could ease the tension from her spirit and calm her soul. Although she had loved Otis dearly, it had been a good long jump since she'd thought about him in that way or had those reflections calm her being.

Miss Jen Pearl wondered a lot about Leah Mosley, the only daughter of Ezra and Bessie Turrentine. Her mother had been a twin, her uncle Leon passing away in nineteen forty-three, just two days before the duos thirty-third birthday. The pair had been born in Port Royal, South Carolina and her grandmother Bessie had called the two a sweet blessing sent straight from heaven to her hands.

Nana Leah had been twenty when she met Benjamin Mosley. Benjamin had been ten years her senior and he'd married her one-week after her twenty-fifth birthday. It was a short four months later when Jen Pearl pushed her way into her mother's heart. Her parents had existed comfortably with one another, but there had been nothing between them that had ever given her any indication that Nana Leah had thought of her father in that special way. Perhaps if she had, Jen Pearl thought, she'd understand why her daughter had clung so to the tall, white man who made butterflies flutter in the pit of her stomach.

From the room at the end of the hall, she could hear her mother calling for her. Calling for Jen Pearl to bring the meal that had been offered just minutes before. Taking a deep inhale, Miss Jen Pearl started the wash cycle, filling the porcelain tub with soap powder and bleach. As she watched the container fill with cold water she pulled the dirty clothes from the floor and dropped the garments inside. Down the hall, her mother screamed louder for her attention.

"Just a minute, Mama," she finally screamed back. "I heard you the first time. I'll be right there."

TWENTY

Graye had barely been twenty years old the first time he spent a night in jail. He'd spent many more after that first time, jail and Graye becoming a common pairing. None of his transgressions had been too serious, until his thirtieth birthday, and then, within a quick, ten-minute span of time, he had been just a shade shy of killing a man. His offense, assault with a deadly weapon, had earned him an eleven-month sentence behind bars and two years of probation.

Graye remembered the moment well, recalling the rage that had danced on the hard wood floors of the Easy Slide Café. His friend Tate had been there to stop him that night. Tate had pulled him off Wallace Baker, loosening the hold he had on Wallace's obese neck, while prying the broken remnants of a table leg from the tight fist Graye had wrapped around the short length of wood.

Graye winced at the memory, remembering how pasty and dough-like Wallace's thick flesh had felt beneath his palms. Stepping on Graye's foot as he'd stumbled in a drunken march had been all

Wallace had done to earn the savage beating Graye had put on him. Stepping on Graye's foot and marring the brand new, cream-colored, alligator shoes on Graye's feet had been the man's crime. When Tate pulled Graye off, Wallace had been left with a broken windpipe, a cracked jaw, a bloody nose, four missing front teeth, and more bruises than anyone was ever able to count. Wallace's mind hadn't been all there before the beating. Afterwards, there wasn't much of anything left to Wallace Baker at all.

Graye eyed the over-weight man curiously as he walked slowly down the narrow street, dragging his feet in the dry dust. The man's body was hunched awkwardly, his shoulders rolled askew, his head hanging low to the ground. His clothes, ill fitting, were more filth than fabric, hanging in tatters around his bloated flesh. Graye watched him as Wallace shuffled slowly from one corner to the other, mumbling incoherently under his breath.

Across the way, his mother called Wallace's name, seemingly excited to see him as she reached her arms out to hug the man close. Wallace appeared to perk up as Miss Jen Pearl spoke to him, his head bobbing up and down excitedly. Graye sneered, wondering what his mother could possibly have to say to the likes of Wallace Baker, the man who'd ruined his new shoes and had caused him to go to jail. In the room behind him, Angelette hummed softly, wiping dust off the furniture with a clean white rag and a can of lemon-scented furniture polish.

Graye turned his attention away from the window and to the woman as she slid the small knickknacks from one side of the tabletop to the other, wiping at the surface beneath them. She hummed, a coy smile gracing her face, her hair pulled back into a neat ponytail that hung down the length of her back. Graye smiled, palming a hand across the front of his crotch and the length of tissue that had twitched with anticipation.

"Why are you so happy?" he asked, breaking the silence between them.

Tossing him a quick glance, Angelette smiled in his direction, shrugging her shoulders. She continued with her chores, not bothering to give him any answer at all.

He gestured to the outside with his head, speaking more to hear his own voice than caring if Angelette was paying him any never mind. "Wallace

Baker over there talking to my mama." He scowled, his gaze moving from the scene outside and back to Angelette. He watched her as she continued with her chores, her thoughts someplace other than there in that room with him. "Come here," Graye commanded, lifting his body from the window seat and dropping down into the low chair that sat in the middle of the room.

A look of reluctance twitched across Angelette's face, but she smiled instead, forcing her lips upward as she crossed the room to his side and sat down against his lap. Graye held her tightly, his arms wrapped like a vise around her midsection. Angelette leaned to press a kiss against his forehead and Graye nodded his approval, the gesture slow and easy. He held her tight and neither of them spoke a word, both drifting in the direction of their own reflections.

Midnight had come and gone as Angelette lay wide-awake waiting for Graye to find his way home. Time ticked, the pace seemingly slower than normal and Angelette blew her frustration out in heavy gales past her full lips. The heavy knock on the front door

surprised her.   Graye had no reason to knock,
knowing the front entrance was never secured, always
open in anticipation of the man's arrival home.   The
knocking continued, persistent, and demanding,
inciting a wave of anxiety to replace the boredom
Angelette had felt only minutes before.

"Who's there?" she called out, lifting her body
from the bed to stand in the center of the room.

The knocking stopped, Tate Butler calling his
name from the other side of the wooden frame. "It's
me, Angelette. I need to speak with you."

Angelette rushed to the door, pulling it open
just wide enough to peer outside. Tate stood with his
hands pushed deep into his pockets. He gave her a
quick smile, the gesture culminating out of sheer
politeness and a flood of anxiety.

"Sorry to wake you, Angelette," he mumbled
softly.

"What's wrong? Where's Graye?"

Tate heaved a deep sigh, pushing his hands
deeper into his pockets. "I'm sorry, Angelette. Graye
got himself thrown into jail tonight. He won't be
coming home for a few days."

Tate's eyes darted around the room behind her head, fighting not to stop on Angelette or meet her intense stare. The man continued talking, nervous energy forming his words.

"Graye got into a fight with Wallace down at the club. He beat him up some sort of bad. Sheriff came and took Graye away. He said we could go down to the courthouse tomorrow to see about the charges. But it's not good, Angelette. Graye beat Wallace real bad. He looked almost dead. Ambulance had to come take the boy to the hospital." Tate sighed, then took a deep inhale, finally allowing his gaze to touch Angelette's face.

Moonlight flickered over the woman's profile. Tate thought she looked angelic standing there as dark shadows danced against the wall behind her and the pale slivers of white light illuminated her face. Her hair lay loose around her shoulders, billowing down in soft curls that framed her face nicely. Her lips were parted ever so slightly, warm breath blowing out into the cool night air. As she stared up at him, her large eyes glistened, and her gaze whispered his name teasingly.

What Tate wanted to say, he couldn't, fighting the sudden urge to pull her slight figure against the hardness of his body as he whispered his longing into the soft curve of her neck. "I'm sorry," he said instead, his voice soft. "You shouldn't have to deal with this mess."

Angelette shrugged, then nodded slowly, not missing the unspoken thoughts that spilled from his eyes. The moment between them was suddenly awkward.

Tate clenched his fists tightly against his legs. "I should be going," he said. "I'll come back in the morning."

Angelette smiled. "It's already morning." Her resonance was low, an enticing, seductive vibrato that brushed a current of heat against his skin.

Tate chuckled nervously. "It is, isn't it?" he responded, his tone teasing hers.

Angelette leaned back against the door, hands clutching the doorknob behind her back. The invitation was unspoken as she opened the door just wide enough for him to enter. Without saying a word, Tate eased himself slowly inside. His temperature rose with a vengeance as his body brushed lightly against hers, the round of her breasts just grazing his left arm. The electricity that shivered through him intensified as Angelette closed and locked the door behind them.

"I've got to finish my cleaning, Graye," Angelette whispered softly. "Then I want to make you a nice dinner," she said as she moved to ease herself up and off his lap.

Graye studied her, his gaze skimming the soft curves of her face. His grip around her waist tightened as he reached one hand to the back of her head pulling her face to his. Pressing his mouth to her mouth, the kiss was almost frantic, an obscene hunger pulling at Angelette's lips. As Graye pushed his tongue into the moist cavity, Angelette fought the sudden urge to heave, bile rising heavy against the back of her throat. Graye could feel the wave of tension that filled her, her sudden desire to push him as far away from her as she could muster. It made him want her even more.

As he broke the connection, Angelette gasped for air, the back of her hand flying up to cover her bruised lips. Graye ignored the rise of tears that suddenly filled his woman's dark eyes. He focused instead on the rise and fall of the breast pressed beneath the palm of his hand. Oblivious to her pain, he kneaded the soft tissue with a heavy hand, his touch purposely brutal. When his gaze finally met hers, the darkness that lay behind his stare was frightening. Angelette's breathing intensified, coming in short gasps, and when Graye tore at the fabric of her blouse, shredding the soft cotton from her body, fear dropped her to the floor at his feet. The blows that followed, Graye's fists pummeling her body, kept her there.

Miss Jen Pearl said nothing as she nursed the bruises her youngest child had inflicted upon his wife. Angelette had been battered black and blue, the rising welts and abrasions marring every part of her except her face. Her face was blemish free, the silk of her skin as beauteous as the day she'd been born. Miss Jen Pearl knew that one had only to look deep into Angelette's eyes though to see the full extent of the damage Graye had caused. Angelette's contusions were soul deep, reaching the pith of her spirit where no amount of salve could soothe its pain.

Behind them, Nana Leah and her granddaughters muttered amongst themselves like a cluck of gossiping hens. The two women stood listening as the others attested to the worthlessness of Graye McAdams, foul-tempered men, and the whole male sex in general. By the time Sister had professed for the third time what she would do if her husband had beat her like that, Miss Jen Pearl had had her fill of all of them.

"Enough," she chastised, almost shouting as her gaze drifted from one surprised face to the other. "I have had just about enough. You girls done worked my last nerve. Ain't you all got some place to go home to that ain't my home?"

July shook her head, her eyes widened as she met her mother's gaze. "We're sorry, Mama. We just wanted to give you a hand with Angelette. We didn't mean no harm."

The matriarch took a deep breath, filling her lungs with air. Beneath the warmth of her palm, Angelette was still shaking as if cold. Nana Leah came to her feet, a pout pulling at her lips.

"Don't need to get hot with me, Jen Pearl. You ain't too grown and I don't care how old you are."

"Go to bed, Mama," Miss Jen Pearl said, her tone commanded. She softened her voice ever so slightly. "You needs some rest. I don't want you feeling poorly tomorrow."

As the older woman made her way out the room, slapping the metal feet of her walker against the wood floors, the McAdams' daughters bid their mother and Angelette goodnight, easing out the front door without uttering another word until they were well out of earshot. Both Angelette and Miss Jen Pearl blew stale air past their lips as they settled into the quiet that their family members had finally left behind. Silence claimed its place, the hum of the refrigerator and the occasional drip from the faucet the only sound. Angelette was only slightly startled when minutes later her mother-in-law finally spoke.

"Where Graye go off to, do you know?"

Angelette shrugged. "Down to the Easy-Slide, I think."

His mother nodded her head as she proceeded to gather up the ointments and bandages, dropping them back into the tin can that she called a medicine kit. Her jaw was tight as she lifted Angelette's chin into the palm of her hand, lifting the woman's gaze up to hers. The two women locked eyes, both noting the rise of tears they willed from falling.

"A man will only do what you let him get away with. And if you let Graye get away with this, he will only do it again," Miss Jen Pearl said, her pronouncement coming with firm conviction as she slowly enunciated each word.

Angelette sputtered, opening and closing her mouth as she struggled to respond. She had no words though, nothing to say that would excuse Graye for what he had done to her, or her for refusing to do something for herself. As Miss Jen Pearl collected the last of her supplies, her comment would be the last one either would make that night. The woman gestured toward the door as she exited the room, cutting off the lights as she made her way. When Angelette had grown weary of sitting alone, in the dark, she wrapped her coat around her shoulders and eased her battle-weary body across the street toward home.

All eyes watched as Graye entered the Easy Slide Café, tossing his hand up at the bartender on duty before taking his usual seat in the back corner. All eyes watched as he settled himself comfortably in the wooden chair, resting his elbows against the tabletop. Reaching into the pocket of his leather jacket, Graye pulled out a pack of Marlboro cigarettes, lit one with a butane lighter, and then nodded as the bartender rested a bottle of Jack Daniel's and an empty glass on the tabletop in front of him. He nodded his appreciation, dropping three twenty-dollar bills into the man's hands.

"That should get me started," he said, his voice barely audible.

The tall, black man, kin to the owner and his family, simply shrugged, nodded, and returned to his station behind the bar. Graye's gaze ran from one corner of the room to the other, noting the two men who sat side by side in front of the jukebox, the three, overly dressed women leaning against the bar, and the couple huddled close at the table across from him. He made eye contact with each one, sending the various stares in the opposite direction, turning their attention far from him and his doings. All eyes turned away, feigning interest in everything else but Graye McAdams.

The bitter fluid felt good as it burned a path across his tongue and down the back of this throat. It took very little, just three quick shots, to ease the tension that pulled at the muscles across his shoulders and along his thick neck. By the fifth shot he had almost forgotten completely the misery that Angelette had brought upon him just hours earlier, the bitter reminder that she had not wanted him. He burned hot with rage each and every time she pulled away from him, cringing with distaste beneath his hand as if there were something wrong with his touch. Reminding him that he really didn't have her love, no matter what words had passed out of her mouth.

He remembered all too well when he'd begun to sense that something was different about Angelette and then things between them had started to change. He'd begun to feel like Angelette's heart longed for something or someone other than him. He'd been all smiles when he'd first come home that first time, his last night in the state penitentiary nothing but a fading memory in his mind. His grin had spanned from one side of his dark face to the other in anticipation of holding Angelette as he dropped himself deep into the chasm of her heart and lingered until both of them were full and satisfied with each other.

The scuffle he'd had with Wallace Baker had taken him away from her for far too long and Graye was more than ready to pick up where the two of them had left off. As he'd stepped off the Greyhound bus he'd looked around anxiously, hoping that she would be there waiting for him. As the other passengers set off toward their final destinations, there had been no one there to greet and welcome him home. He had walked the last leg of his trip, traveling the two miles to the dirt road he'd been raised on and the small cottage that he and Angelette called home.

His mother had been in her front yard as he'd approached, kneeling as if in prayer as she'd fussed and preened a newly planted garden of plastic, dime-store blooms. He'd dropped to the ground beside her and had offered up half an apology for the crime that had caused a slight hitch in his life. Miss Jen Pearl had appealed to him to go and offer the fat, doughboy an apology for his behavior and after a half-hearted promise, he'd headed across the street toward home.

Tate Butler had stepped out of his front door just seconds before he'd reached his hand out to turn the knob.

The two men both stepped back, for a brief moment, stunned by the shock and surprise of bumping into the other. Graye's eyes narrowed ever so slightly as his gaze shifted past Tate's shoulder and fell on Angelette who'd stepped up behind the man. She smiled widely as Tate spoke first.

"Graye, hey man. We was just coming to the bus stop to pick you up." Tate looked down to the watch on his wrist. "You got in early."

Graye shrugged. "Yeah. I guess I did. What you doin' here?"

Tate pulled his full lips into a slight smile as he gave his friend a quick hug. He stepped back out of Graye's space as he spoke. "I just came by to pick up Angelette. We both wanted to be there to welcome you home."

As Tate spoke her name, Angelette eased from behind the man, her arms extended as she reached to embrace Graye. She reached up on the tips of her toes to kiss his cheek, moving her mouth around to his lips. "I missed you, Graye," she whispered softly, allowing her body to ease against his.

Graye pulled her close and kissed her back. Hard. His lips strangling hers as his body demanded her full attention. When he finally let her go, bristling as she stepped away and out of his reach, he could feel the sudden rise of awkward tension that had filled the empty space between them. It was like a rash, begging to be scratched as it spread itself in search of attention. Tate smiled at him and then her, the look in his eyes one Graye had never seen before.

"Well," Tate started, "I guess I'll be going home. Let you two be alone again."

"You don't have to leave," Angelette said, her tone anxious. "We can have us a drink to celebrate Graye coming home. And I made some dinner. You more than welcome to come eat with us." She smiled at her husband, her eyes widening as if she were begging him to agree with her. Graye said nothing at all, shifting a stare back and forth between the two of them.

Tate stared back at the man as if waiting for a response, sensing that Graye had no intentions of giving him one. He winked at his friend. "Thanks for the invitation, Angelette, but you and Graye need some time alone. Me and Graye can catch up at the club later on. What you say, Graye?"

Graye smiled, the saccharine of it like poison. "What you hurrying off for? Come on in and sit a spell. Catch me up on everything that's been going on. What you cook, Angelette?"

"Made your favorite. Fried chicken and potato salad. Your mama helped me."

He nodded his head as the trio made their way inside. Looking about the small space, he noted that very little had changed. Everything was neatly in its place and Angelette had even adorned the kitchen table with a vase of fresh flowers purchased from the local grocery store. Tate stood awkwardly until Graye gestured toward the oversized recliner and told him to take a seat.

As Angelette moved toward the kitchen area, Graye grabbed her by the wrist. He pulled her toward the bathroom as he tossed a quick gaze over his shoulder at Tate.

"We be right back. Just make yourself at home," he said.

Behind the closed door, he wrapped his arms tightly around the woman's waist. "How much you miss me?" he asked, peering intently into her eyes.'

Angelette giggled. "I missed you a lot, Graye. You know that."

He nodded slowly as he dropped his mouth to hers, kissing her softly. As his tongue moved to part her lips, licking at the line of her teeth, Angelette pressed the flat of her palms against his broad chest and pushed him away.

"You hungry, Graye?" she asked as her eyes shifted from side to side, refusing to meet his stare.

He shook his head.

"We should probably go back out," Angelette whispered. "We do have company."

When she moved to ease her body past him, Graye swung her back around, his expression tensing with annoyance. "He can wait. Ain't like he special."

There was a flicker of something ugly that crossed the man's face and Angelette eyed him with reservation. She smiled again, nodding ever so slightly. Graye pulled a large hand through the length of her hair, his palm pressed against the back of her head as he kissed her again. Before Angelette realized what was happening, Graye had spun her around, bending her over the bathroom sink as he pressed her face against the mirror. He reached a large hand beneath her skirt and pulled aside the panel of fabric that covered her crotch. She gasped loudly as his thick fingers bore into her, Graye mauling her flesh as if he'd lost something deep in the moist cavity. Before she could blow the breath back out Graye had entered her from behind, the length of him filling the space his fingers had just vacated.

"Graye, don't," Angelette had implored, the loud whisper seeming to incite further fury. The woman struggled beneath the weight of him as he pounded his body harshly into hers. "Please...Graye...wait, please...," she sputtered, as she struggled to make sense of the moment, Graye's fury and insistence in full control.

"You forgot who you belong to," Graye answered, growling into her ear. "To hell with waiting," he cursed.

Staring at her reflection, Angelette said nothing else. This was surely not how she'd planned their reunion. The fantasy of candlelight and soft music, Graye staring into her eyes and the two of them giggling like they'd done before he'd left had dissipated into thin air. Gone as if it had never been there at all. Graye met her gaze, his eyes locking with hers in the reflection of the mirror. There was something horrific that creased the lines of his face as he grunted his passion, still ramming his body harshly into hers. Graye called her names, ugly, vile enumerations that rang as harshly against her ears as the assault on her body. Profanity spewed like venom through the air, sweeping through the hollow-core door into the other room.

On the other side, Tate rose from his seat and eased his way across the room and out of the house. Pausing only briefly, he pulled the door closed behind him, securing it tightly. Before heading back across town to his own home, he stopped to say hello to Miss Jen Pearl.

Graye shook the memory from his mind, taking a quick glance around the room. He tossed back the last drops of drink in his glass and gestured toward the bartender to bring him another bottle of Jack. The room had filled quickly, a crowd of familiar faces having gathered to party through the late night. When the front door opened for the umpteenth time, Graye didn't even bother to look up, not caring who had come through the entrance. Not even the growing quiet around him was enough to bring him to lift his head to peer up at the space around him.

But the room had gone quiet, laughter and the hushed whispers of conversation dropping into a lull of silence. The man in the blue uniform who stood at his elbow was Graye's first hint that the remainder of his evening had surely gone straight to hell. The other tapping him against his shoulder was the second. Grayed heaved a deep sigh as he finally looked up, his gaze moving from one to the other.

"What?" he asked, his speech only slightly slurred. "What I do now?"

"Are you Graye McAdams?" the taller, blonde-haired man asked.

Graye shrugged. "You know I am," he answered, his annoyance like a thick phlegm in his mouth. "Everybody know who I am," he said, irritated that the fool had even bothered to ask.

The man continued. "Mr. McAdams, you're under arrest. Please put your hands behind your back."

Graye bristled, then chuckled under his breath. "That's funny," he said. "What you arresting me for now?"

The uniformed black man responded. "Domestic violence, Mr. McAdams. You're under arrest for the assault against you wife. Now," the man said, his stance stiffening, "put your hands behind your back."

Graye squinted as if the man had shouted in his ear, the harshness of it ringing through his head. "Assault? I ain't do nothin' to that woman," he professed. "I wouldn't hurt, Angelette."

Graye could make out the words of his Miranda Rights as the law enforcement officer clasped a pair of handcuffs around his wrists. The sound of them wove an intricate pattern between his thoughts of Angelette and his astonishment that someone had actually called the police on him, butting into business that should have stayed private between him and his wife.

TWENTY-ONE

Doc Burton had kissed her at the bus station, pressing his thin lips against the lush fullness of her own. His touch had been shaky and Miss Jen Pearl couldn't help but wonder if it had been due to the man's old age or sheer nervousness. His mouth had lingered like silk against her lips, his palm lightly grazing the side of her face. The feel of his fingertips just at the edge of her eyes still burned hot and Miss Jen Pearl inhaled swiftly at the memory, her palm falling to the flutter of energy that pierced her abdomen. Angelette tossed her a quick look, her eyes misting as if they shared a semblance of understanding, then she smiled and turned to stare back off in the other direction.

Jen Pearl would never be able to explain what had possessed her to buy the two bus tickets to Charleston. There had been no thought of it at all when she'd opened her eyes that morning. Her day had started like all the others, the alarm clock on the nightstand chiming at precisely five o'clock. Then the old dog that was her mother's pet, but slept at the foot of her bed and followed behind Jen Pearl during the day had pressed his wet nose against the palm of her hand begging to be let outside. She'd risen like always, slipping on her tattered slippers and the flannel house coat that felt good against her skin before making her way to the back door to unlock the latch and let the day begin.

Minutes later a pot of coffee was brewing in the percolator and the first hint of a morning sun had begun to peek over the horizon, waving a lazy hand for her attention. Like always, Jen Pearl had stepped out onto her front porch, still wrapped in her housecoat, a cup of that hot coffee in her hand. She'd taken a moment to mutter a quick prayer of thanks for a new day and then had looked across the street to see if her son was coming in or going out. This morning though, there had been no sign of Graye, not even his car parked in the driveway. The call came some five hours later as the first load of laundry was being pulled from the washer and carried to the clothesline that hung from the corner of the small house out to the large oak tree that shaded the center of the yard.

Graye had called in want of money, needing someone to call Drake Tyler and come post the bond he knew the law would impose upon them before they'd set him free. Miss Jen Pearl had only nodded into the receiver, not bothering to answer her child who was begging for her help. As Graye had cried, appealing to her maternal instincts, she had suddenly thought of Charleston. She had never been to Charleston before. Otis had never allowed her to go.

As she settled herself comfortably in the seat, waving her good-bye toward Doc and her daughters, Miss Jen Pearl mused that she couldn't remember if she had even bothered to tell her son good-bye before she'd dropped the receiver back onto the hook. She had told him she loved him she recalled, nodding her head as the memory wafted through her mind, but that was all she'd had to say to him, hanging up the phone as if he hadn't called at all.

Knowing there would be no second call from her wayward son, she'd gone to check on Nana Leah. The old woman had been muttering an all too familiar tune and in the blink of an eye, Jen Pearl had made the decision to pack up herself, and Angelette, to search out that spot where the sand kissed the water. And so she'd packed her bags first, and when she'd been finished had called for the doctor and her daughters to come as soon as they could. Across the street, she had entered the newly cleaned home and had smiled as Angelette had stood staring at her, not knowing what else to do. As she had packed a bag for Angelette, neither of them had spoken a word. Angelette had followed like a small child, Miss Jen Pearl leading her out her front door by the hand, the small overnight bag tucked securely beneath her arm. Doc Burton had been waiting for them in his car, the vehicle idling in the drive. And now, here it was, not quite half past noon and the two women were on a bus, running as far from home as either had ever imagined going.

It was Angelette's hurt that had awakened Jen Pearl's sleeping demons, willing them alive again. The volatile relationship between her son and the young woman had been the catalyst for pumping oxygen back into the incubus that she had slain and buried years before, resuscitating every ounce of evil back into it that they could muster. Jen Pearl leaned against the bus window, her forehead pressed into the glass as she stared out at the traffic that zipped in slow motion down the extended length of highway.

The memories burned ugly in the pit of her stomach, coating her intestine much like the milky antacid that tasted chalky from the bottle to her mouth. Like the torrid taste of medicine intended to calm the burn that haunted her midsection, the memories were hard to swallow, catching instead in the back of her throat as if preparing to be spewed back out.

Otis hadn't always been an easy man to love. Most times it had been damn hard to give a care about Otis McAdams. On more than one occasion, she had questioned what she felt for him, walking dead center along that fine line that lingered between love and hate. But deep down she had loved Otis, had loved him from the first moment she saw him, when he'd eased into the seat beside her at Mt. Moriah Baptist Church, filling the pew with his thick body. She'd barely been sixteen years old herself, still as innocent as the day her mother had given birth to her and if it were possible, even more naive. She should have known better when he'd leaned in close to her, allowing his leg to brush up against hers and had propositioned her, whispering words into her ear that had nothing to do with praising Jesus or atoning for his many transgressions. She should have publicly execrated him right there that third Sunday, the Sunday the senior choir was boring them with song. Instead, the heat of his breath against her ear had sent a shiver straight through her. It had been as if her mind had turned to sheer mush, the tremor in her thighs taking her by the hand and willing her to sniff behind Otis McAdams as if he'd been a bitch in heat.

Otis had been overly charming and just shy of crude, a lethal combination for a girl with no experience with the male sex. He was the epitome of masculine prowess, a bad boy like no other bad boy, the essence of it oozing from every pore. He'd had an incredible smile that had filled his dark face with a sensual vibrancy, deep hollows dimpling his full cheeks. Life had shimmered like diamonds in his eyes and when he'd looked at her, Jen Pearl hadn't been any more good. He'd towered above her, his large body shadowing her petite frame and he'd been a man who knew how to use his hands. He'd had incredible hands, long, perfectly proportioned fingers and clean nails. From the very beginning, the appendages had constantly touched and pulled and teased and stroked, and usually in places they had no business being.

But like his son, Otis had a dark side, his own demons plaguing his enthralling spirit when Jen Pearl had least expected it. There had been much about the man that she hadn't known. Deep, dark secrets that had been unspoken or unheard of during their short courtship, rearing an ugly head well after her first baby and the commitment of marriage she had engulfed herself in. But there had been one thing about Otis McAdams that Jen Pearl had known without question and no matter how bad things could get between them, she'd grown to trust it.

Otis McAdams had loved her. He had loved her with every fiber in his body, the emotion swelling thick and full until it had become a bitter obsession around them. When Otis had opened his heart to her, he'd claimed her, marking every inch of her as he'd deemed her his personal property, the private territory that only he would ever occupy. Jen Pearl could never imagine any other man loving her as hard, or as deeply, as Otis had claimed to love her. Even at his worst, Jen Pearl believed that Otis' love had been the cause of all his hurtful behavior because only a love so intense could move the human spirit to say and do things a sensible mind would know better than do. Shaking the thoughts from her mind, Miss Jen Pearl heaved another deep sigh, pulling her body up straight in the seat as she reached for the brown paper bag that sat in her lap.

"Are you hungry, Baby Doll? I fixed us some food to eat if you hungry," she said, turning her attention to Angelette.

The young woman shrugged her shoulders, but said nothing. She'd not had much of anything to say since she'd arrived all beaten and bruised on Miss Jen Pearl's doorstep the day before.

Miss Jen Pearl reached into the oversized canvas sack that rested on the floor between her feet. She searched by touch, her fingers sifting through the bag's contents while her gaze remained locked on Angelette's face. A moment later she pulled two sandwiches from an inner pocket and passed one to Angelette.

"Here," she said. "It's peanut butter and grape jelly." She smiled widely, the gesture flooding her face with warmth.

Angelette smiled back as she reached for the Saran-wrapped packet. She toyed with the wrapper as Miss Jen Pearl took a hearty bite out of her own sandwich. Angelette chuckled softly. "Miss Jen Pearl, you don't like peanut butter and jelly," she said softly.

The older woman laughed. "That's not true. I just never fixed it for myself. Otis didn't like it and 'cause he wouldn't eat it, none of my children ever did." She took another bite, chewed and swallowed. "Actually, I love me some peanut butter and jelly. Use to eat it all the time when I was little and mama would can up some of her preserves. She use to make her own peanut butter, too. Fresh. I also like me some I-talian food, chitlins, collard greens, and chocolate cake. But Otis ain't never liked none of the stuff I liked so we just never ate none of it." Miss Jen Pearl shrugged her shoulders casually as she licked a spot of Welch's grape jelly from her fingertip. "My goodness!" she exclaimed suddenly. "We sure 'nuff done give up some stuff for those men of ours!" She paused for a quick minute as if to allow the pronouncement to take hold of them both, digging in its heels to insure they knew and understood the truth of it. "Well, that ends right here, right now," she concluded, tasting the last bite of her sandwich and balling up the wrapper between the palms of her hands. "We ain't giving up nothing else in this life, Baby Doll. Not one more thing!"

Angelette nodded, her head bobbing quickly up and down as she took a bite of her own meal. She smiled again, savoring the taste of it as if it were her first experience with peanut butter. Miss Jen Pearl passed her a bottle of water retrieved from the same canvas bag and then the two women drifted back into their own thoughts.

The bus was filled to capacity, every seat occupied. Across the aisle from them two men sat in deep conversation, their whispers hushed as they worked to keep what was being said from prying ears. One man's hand rested on his companion's thigh, his palm kneading the other's flesh. His touch appeared to be less than gentle. Miss Jen Pearl stared openly at the duo. They seemed to be at odds with one another, their conversation more of a disagreement than anything else. *Don't matter much what the coupling,* she mused to herself. *Couples were always having a time with each other.* She shook her head from side to side.

Behind them a young child sat humming to himself, his mother reading from a storybook that nestled in her lap. Every few minutes the little boy would kick the back of Miss Jen Pearl's seat, his tiny sneakers hitting the deep blue cushion as he swung his legs back and forth. When it finally got on her nerves she lifted herself up to peer over the top of the seat.

"Baby, don't kick my seat now. That ain't polite."

The mother, a young white woman with flaming red hair and a milky complexion bristled slightly, then smiled nervously. Her hand fell to her child's legs to still the quick up and down lift of his legs.

"Don't you be a bother to no one now, Earl James," she said softly, glancing quickly to see if others were witnessing the conversation.

The child looked from one face to another and smiled shyly as he shifted his small body back against the seat.

"I'm sorry about that," the woman volunteered, trying to read the expression that graced Miss Jen Pearl's face.

Miss Jen Pearl smiled again, reaching into the pocket of her polyester jacket and pulling out a cherry-flavored lollipop. She gestured toward the mother first, seeking permission before she handed it to the child.

"I surely appreciate that, baby," she said. "My old back can't take but so much commotion."

The little boy grinned and his mother seemed to heave a grateful sigh that there would be no more problems with her child before the ride to where ever it was they were headed was through. As she settled back down, Miss Jen Pearl tapped her palm against the back of Angelette's fist, the woman's hand clenched tightly in her lap. Angelette looked over at her, moisture shimmering in her gaze as if she wanted to cry.

"We need to go find ourselves, Angelette," she pronounced, speaking as if there had been no lull in their conversation. "Me and you, Baby Doll. We need to go find ourselves, otherwise we ain't gonna be no good for nothing."

Both women turned to stare out the window and Angelette fought back the sudden urge to cry, willing her tears to come no further than the edge of her eyes.

Angelette stretched the length of her body against the cushioned seat. Beside her, Miss Jen Pearl was dozing comfortably. Angelette's gaze shifted around the bus' interior, lingering here and there on the other passengers. It darted back and forth as she willed herself wide-eyed and awake, then returned back to stare past the top of Miss Jen Pearl's head and out the window. She'd lost all sense of time, wondering just how long it had been since fate had tipped her hand and spun her in a whole other direction. She heaved a deep sigh, blowing a gale of nervousness past her pink-toned lips.

Since Graye had thrown that first punch, she'd been trying to figure out the precise moment destiny had betrayed her, spinning her head first into the bowels of hell, bypassing the front door to purgatory all together. Each and every time she'd tried to pinpoint the exact moment, she couldn't help but think that the moment of her birth had probably been her moment of reckoning. There was something so pathetically sad about that thought though that she could only shake her heat at the absurdity of it and smile.

Maybe life had thrown more salt than sugar her way, but she was still here, still standing, and that had to count for something in someone's book, she mused. She heaved another sigh and wondered if every woman had a moment where she reaches the apex of tolerance and she snaps. Hard. By the time Graye had thrown that last punch, Angelette had been on the down hill slide of her point of no return and she had snapped. It wasn't until Miss Jen Pearl had uttered her one and only comment that Angelette had realized just how through with Graye McAdams she truly was. The only problem, she pondered, was whether or not Graye intended to be through with her.

How had she gotten to this place? When the two of them had come together it had been as if Graye had been the answer to prayers that had been ignored for so long before. Graye had been her rock, a boulder of strength that she had come to depend on. And then it all changed. She had changed and she had needed more. More than Graye'd had to give and more than the few stones and pebbles he had allowed her to have.

The old woman stirred beside her, one eye opening to look over at Angelette.

"You ain't sleep?" Miss Jen Pearl asked softly.

"No, ma'am."

The woman nodded as she shifted in her seat, swiping the film from her eyes with the back of her hand. "Where are we?" she asked, looking down to the length of highway that rolled past the window. Cars were speeding beside them, moving like colorful bugs from lane to lane. The sun was still shining brightly, a sweltering wave of heat consuming the air outside. Inside the bus, the driver had turned the air-conditioning up full blast and it blew cold from the vents above their heads.

Angelette shrugged, not knowing anything other than she was glad to be going where ever it was life intended to take her. Her mother-in-law seemed to understand that and so she said nothing else as she folded her arms across her chest, content herself to be without a whole lot of details and specifics that needed to be thought out and planned around.

Miss Jen Pearl suddenly laughed. Anxiously, she patted her hand against Angelette's thigh as if she needed to get the other woman's attention and pointed out the window, the line of her finger waving excitedly at the **Welcome to Charleston** sign.

TWENTY-TWO

Graye had come to understand that no one was coming for him. Two days had passed and there had been no sign of his mother, nothing from Angelette, and his siblings had made it clear that they could care less if he rotted away for what they all believed he had done. But Drake Tyler had earned his keep, meriting the retainer Graye had needed to pay him for his services. The others would see that no matter who had gotten him into this predicament, he would surely see his own way out of it. He always did. Alone. Not needing any help from any of them. And in less than twenty-four hours he would be a free man. Again. Needing only to top off his account with attorney Tyler before finishing what had been started.

Before this, Tate had been the only one who had ever come to his defense, without fail, bailing him out of jail and praying him out of damnation when he'd felt it necessary. Graye couldn't help but laugh at the memories. Tate had been a damn fool, thinking there was something good in Graye worth saving, when deep down in his soul he'd known that the opposite had been the truth. There wasn't anything good about Graye. Not one damn thing. Graye had never tried to hide the truth of himself. It had always been exposed and open for all to see. Tate had just chosen to ignore what was right in front of his face, determined not to believe the ugly of it all. Graye had been the only thing in his life Tate hadn't been able to fix. Graye had been too broken to be repaired by anyone.

Graye rolled onto his stomach, pushing his weight up onto his forearms and toes in a series of push-ups and planks. His muscles were taut, pulling one against the other with nervous energy. He needed out. He needed to feel fresh air against his skin, the caress of a cool breeze teasing his flesh. He yearned to sit beneath the light of a full moon, to watch the shadows that danced and played across his dark skin as images of past and present swept the still night air. He needed to reclaim himself, the him that didn't apologize for who and what he was. The him that didn't have to pretend to be more or who struggled to be what Tate had been. He needed to bury the facade, the pretext of a man who hadn't failed his family or who had cared about another soul or believed he could be different or had wanted more for himself. He yearned for that part of himself that didn't really give a damn. The him that cursed it all, and them, to hell and back.

And he needed to finish what he should have finished the night he killed Tate. He needed to end the torment, to still the quiver of rage that was fighting to control him. He needed to make Angelette pay for what she had done to him and his best friend. For coming between him and his mother. She needed to pay for taking her love and leaving him empty. Angelette needed to pay, to atone for her sins, and his, so that he could be whole again. He only wanted to be whole again and Angelette still held on to far too much of his heart for that to happen.

Pain ripped a short trail up his forearm as he slammed his fist into the cement wall. Skin peeled in a thin layer from his knuckles, the bones just shy of fracturing from the impact. Graye inhaled the hurt of it, relishing the life it infused within him. No one but Tate would have understood and Tate was gone, because of her. The memories of his friend seemed to rise from no where, painting the walls of his cell in want of his attention.

Thirty days. The judge had pronounced the sentence as easily as he'd said his own name. The charge had been disturbing the peace and trespassing. Graye had pled guilty and the sentence had been thirty days. It had rolled off the white man's tongue, past his thin lips and swelled like stale air through the courthouse, barely stopping to slap Graye to attention. Tate had hung his head, his chin falling to his chest as he inhaled the stink of it, allowing it to fill his lungs before blowing it back out. Graye had only laughed, tossing his friend a quick look before the sheriff had tightened the handcuffs around his thick wrists and had guided him out the room.

Two days later Tate was his first visitor. His only visitor. Tate maneuvered his way past the gates, the iron doors, the requisite check-in desk, and the guards who greeted him with indifference. Tate came bearing things he knew Graye would want: cigarettes, magazines, a few Hershey chocolate bars, and a letter from Angelette. They had gathered in a room of other inmates and visitors, mothers and wives and family with fake smiles plastered on frightened faces. Eyes heavy with tears that wouldn't fall, and anger that floated just beneath the surface because there were better things to do on a Saturday morning than visit criminals who'd lost their souls. Better places to be than there, in the thick of so many stagnant bodies. And Tate had come, smiling, happy, hopeful, that this time would be the last time. That Graye would see his way clear to do his thirty days and never again have to do time.

"Yo' buddy, how's it hanging?" Tate asked, dropping into a chair on one side of the wooden table.

Graye shrugged his broad shoulders, pushing them toward the ceiling. "You know how it is. How's things with you?"

Tate grinned again. "Nothing new going on. Had to come check on you. Make sure you doing okay."

"I'm doing."

Tate nodded his head slowly, his eyes flickering to the tables beside them. His gaze lingered on the middle aged woman with the cocoa complexion who wore too much make up and too few clothes. She caught him staring and she crossed her bare legs suggestively, her palm dropping to the inner curve of her equally bare breast. Tate blinked away his embarrassment as his gaze skated quickly away.

He stopped to stare at a little girl with blonde curls and skin the color of freshly fallen snow. She was pale, eerily so, and she seemed to be petrified of the old man in the prison-issued jumpsuit who had her same blue eyes. When his eyes finally met Graye's for a second time, they both nodded, not sure what to say or if anything needed to be said at all.

"What Angelette have to say?" Graye finally asked, leaning back in the wooden chair, his hands clasped casually in his lap.

"She just wanted to make sure you got her letter. She's missing you. Wants you to hurry and come home."

"She say that?"

Tate nodded. "She said she misses you."

Graye allowed another waft of silence to spin between them, his eyes still locked firmly on his friend.

"Angelette like telling you things. She don't talk to me like she talk to you."

Tate shrugged. "She tries. But you always too busy to listen. You just need to relax and just let it happen. You love her and she loves you. You two can work through anything together."

Graye stared at the expanse of the wooden table before him. He followed the grain of the oak-stained wood with his eyes, connecting the lines as if he were playing one of those psychological tests they gave him each time he came and went from this place. His mind was mulling over Tate's comments, allowing the words to rise and fall with thoughts that had nothing to do with anything at all. When he finally spoke, he didn't recognize the voice that whispered past his thick lips. Didn't know the words were his until they'd been spoken aloud and clear.

"You ain't never gone have her. You know that, don't you?" Graye pronounced, his deep voice barely audible as he shifted forward, leaning across the table toward his friend. "Never. I won't ever let you have her."

Tate closed his eyes and inhaled, swallowing a thick breath of air before looking back to his friend. He shook his head.

"Angelette loves you, Graye. You know it. And so do I. You're my best friend, my brother. So don't start this again. Not now."

Graye smiled, his lips bending upward, the gesture coming with an evil awkwardness. It was out of place against the backdrop of anger that lined Graye's expression, hostility dancing in the coldness of his eyes. Nothing about his smile seemed to belong there, in that moment, between the two of them. Graye shifted his body back against his seat.

"You love her, "he said, just a hint of query to his statement. "You love her and you want her," he repeated, thinking he were asking when clearly he wasn't.

He didn't need to wait for an answer. He saw it on Tate's face, in his eyes, the truth of it painting his expression. He saw it when Tate shifted his gaze to stare across the way, his eyes dancing on the blank wall behind his head. He had always seen it, had known it was there since that first time when Tate had first met Angelette, filling her head with things that were his things. Things that didn't include Graye. He saw the raw emotion of it on Tate's expression and recognized it for what it was, what it had been for longer than he had been willing to admit. He knew it as well as he knew his own name having seen it before on Angelette's face and hearing it in her voice. It had slept in his bed, had fed him his meals, and washed his clothes. It had existed for longer than he should have allowed it, its residency filling up space that should only have been his, that he had laid claim to and had been denied.

He stood up, pausing as Tate shifted his focus upward to stare at him. When Tate came to his own feet, meeting Graye eye to eye, Graye saw how things would eventually end for them all. It flashed in bold color before him, the spatter of sanguine fluid, brilliant and red painting the picture for him to see. It was tangible, blooming thick and full of life in the silence that they'd fallen into.

Graye extended his hand and Tate shook it. In that one moment they were just two friends saying good-bye, wishing the other well until the next time. In that split second Graye clasped Tate's fingers tightly, knowing there would never again be a next time when they would truly be friends.

Graye smiled his hatred for a second time. "But I trust you," he concluded, his tone devoid of any true emotion. "You're my best friend. If a man can't trust his best friend with his woman who can he trust," he said softly and then he turned, heading back through the door he'd come in. Tate had stood staring after him longer than had been necessary and as Graye had made his way back to his cell, he'd chalked off another hour, another minute, twenty-eight more days of time before he'd be going home. Twenty-eight more days before it all would end.

Graye heaved a deep sigh as he pressed his back against the wall, allowing his palms to fall against the stone partition. The concrete was cold and harsh against the tips of his fingers. Twenty-eight days had come and gone and then Tate had been dead. The memories flashed like snap shots through Graye's mind. Tate was gone and now he only had twenty-one hours before he'd be free just one last time to finish what he'd started.

TWENTY-THREE

Miss Jen Pearl imagined they looked out of place as they strolled barefoot down the length of sandy beach. Clouds had filled the sky the day before, announcing an impending rain with gale-force winds. The air was damp and chilly, moisture misting down out of the sky, and though there was no sign of any summer sunshine, she and Angelette had spent the entire day straddling the line where the edge of the ocean blue water and the land held hands.

There hadn't been much for either of them to say. There had been no words for the wealth of emotions that had consumed them. Angelette had cried, bawling like a baby. Tears of joy had spilled down her cheeks as she had dropped to her knees to play in the sand, the rush of foam-capped water dancing over her bare feet and legs. And even as Jean Pearl had watched her, there still had been no tears of her own to spill. But she had dropped down beside the girl, water soaking through her cotton shift and she had played too. Together they had built castles out of the wet sand and then had watched in silence as the rising waves had reclaimed what rightfully belonged back in the ocean.

Angelette had danced, spinning her body in circles, her arms outstretched at her sides. She had been a sight to behold, the fabric of her sheer white sundress clinging to her body. The length of her long, lean legs and the round of her buttocks had been exposed as the skirt of her dress had spun out around her. A man walking a large white dog had stopped to watch her, a wistful gaze seeping from bright blue eyes. When Miss Jen Pearl had met his stare with one of her own, he had only smiled, contrition pulling at his expression as if he needed to apologize for the salacious thoughts that had swept through his mind. As Miss Jen Peal had watched him, as he had watched Angelette, she could only imagine what perverse images had been spinning around through his head. Personally, she would have just thought them both crazy, an old black woman and a young black girl acting the fool beneath a cloud-filled sky. When Angelette had finally dropped back down to the ground, her arms and legs flailing against the sand in her efforts to make a sand angel, he had thrown his head back and had laughed, him and his dog finally moving on to finish their walk.

Angelette stood back up, staring down at her handiwork. A broad grin filled her face, satisfaction gleaning from her eyes. She skipped off, searching for seashells that had washed ashore, rushing back to drop them in Miss Jen Pearl's lap. Her excitement was infectious and when she laughed, the beauty of it echoing off in the distance, Miss Jen Pearl had laughed with her. Time danced with them, spinning the women from one end of the beach to the other. Eventually, Angelette sat back down, settling herself beside Miss Jen Pearl. The two women sat content, watching as the spray of the ocean washed up and over their feet, seeping between their toes.

"Did you love him?" Angelette suddenly asked, turning to stare at her mother-in-law. "Did you love your husband?"

Miss Jen Pearl stared out over the skyline, imagining how exquisite the sun must look when it settled down over the horizon, dropping low in the sky and disappearing behind the edge of the ocean. Blue sky kissing blue water, the bright rays of yellow and orange caressing them both. She shrugged her shoulders and answered honestly.

"Only when I had to," she answered softly. "Only when I had to."

"But you stayed with him. You would still be with him if he was alive, wouldn't you?"

The old woman nodded. "Yes," she said firmly. "I would. I would have done what was right for my family, for my children."

Angelette nodded her head slowly, bending her knees up toward her chest as she dug her toes into the coarse grains of sand. "What about you? Didn't you deserve to be happy?" she asked, cutting her eye toward Miss Jen Pearl.

"I was happy."

"But you could have been happier. You had Doc Burton and he loved you. He still loves you. You could have been so much happier."

"I don't know that."

"Yes, you do," the young woman said curtly. Miss Jen Pearl heaved a deep sigh. "Maybe, but sitting here thinking about would-a's, could-a's and should-a's ain't gone change nothing. What's done is done," she said, resolve coating her words.

Angelette leaned her cheek down against her knees, turning her head to stare at Miss Jen Pearl. She wrapped her arms around her legs, hugging herself tightly. "Did you and Doc Burton ever..." the girl paused as her mother-in-law turned to stare back at her. "I mean," she continued, "when you was still with Daddy Otis, did you and Doc ever...?"

Miss Jen Pearl chuckled softly, the length of her gray hair waving from side to side as it swept over her shoulders and across her back. "No. Never," she answered.

"But you wanted to?"

"Yes."

"And you didn't?"

"Not once."

"Why?"

For a quick moment Miss Jen Pearl was at a loss for an answer. She pondered the question, her eyes skipping out over the landscape as she focused on nothing in particular. Her senses seemed heightened, she thought, as the smell of salt water filled the air around her, seeming to filter through her pores and deep into her body. She could taste it, salt like bile filling her mouth, tainting the back of her throat, and upsetting her stomach. The roar of the high seas was suddenly harsh against her ears, the heavy waves beating a hard rhythm against the land. She thought about Doc Burton and the passing of time between them.

There was a loud banging on her front door. Jen Pearl had risen from her bed to go see who was knocking. The house was empty, her children off to some church function with her mother. She had no idea where Otis had gone off to. On the other side of the door, Horace Burton stood anxiously. His blond hair swayed into his eyes and he brushed it from his sight as he peeked through the panes of glass hoping that Jen Pearl was at home.

Jen Pearl had peeked out the window, spying the man who stood anxiously. He was dressed casually in tan khakis and a red plaid shirt. She watched as he walked the length of the front porch, taking the steps two by two as he moved round to the back of the house, searching the yard, and then back up to the front door. He knocked again, this time calling out her name.

She opened it slowly, her eyes wide with curiosity. The tall, white man grinned broadly at the sight of her.

"Jen Pearl, I was just about to leave," he said breathlessly. "Is everything alright?"

Jen Pearl nodded. "It is. I was just taking a quick nap while I had some peace and quiet."

He nodded, then gestured with his head. "May I come in? I saw Otis going into the bar downtown and I know your mother is down at the church. I was hoping I'd find you here alone."

Jen Pearl hesitated, then stepped back, opening the door wide enough for him to enter. As he stepped past her, the scent of his light cologne filled her nostrils. She inhaled, her breath catching deep in her chest and she held it, her gaze following him as he turned to stare at her. Dr. Burton smiled, his hands twisting nervously in front of him.

"What are you doing here?" Jen Pearl asked, finally exhaling. "You know you shouldn't be here, Horace."

He nodded. "I know. I just needed to see you, Jen Pearl." He stepped in toward her, his hands falling to the thin line of her waist. "I missed you."

Jen Pearl stepped out of his grasp, visibly flustered by the warmth of his touch. "Go home, Horace. Please. You know I can't do this."

The man shook his head. "I know. I just..."

Jen Pearl held up her hand to stall his comment. She shook her head, then peeked past the length of lace curtain to the outside. She looked up and down the road, searching for any sight of Otis or her mother, then spun back around to face the man. As she did, Horace stepped back toward her, pulling her body against his as he wrapped his arms around her. He kissed her, his thin lips soft and gentle against her own. Jen Pearl fell into the embrace and kissed him back. When his tongue searched out hers, his hands gliding down the length of her body, she pulled away, clutching at the front of her housecoat. Tears filled her eyes.

"Don't, Jen Pearl. Don't cry. Please," Horace whispered, his palm caressing the side of her face.

"You can't keep doing this to me, Horace. You can't."

He squeezed his eyes shut, his head waving slightly from side to side. "Why, Jen Pearl? I love you. I know you love me. I know you want me as much as I want you. I know you do."

She shook her head vehemently. "I love Otis, Horace. Otis is my husband."

The man bristled. "You don't love him. Not like you love me. You know you don't."

"He's my husband. And you have a wife. You know you and I can never cross that line. Never. So go home, Horace. Go home before we do something we both regret. Go home while I still have the strength to let you go. Please!"

Horace heaved a deep sigh. His eyes dampened with moisture.

"Please," Jen Pearl begged as she pressed her palms against his chest, her own tears beginning to drip down her cheeks.

"Just tell me the truth first," Horace said, his voice barely a whisper. "I have to know the truth," he implored.

Jen Pearl nodded her head, stepping back against him. She lifted her mouth to his and kissed him one more time. His heart raced beneath her fingers, racing to catch up to the beat of her own heart. Horace clasped her cheeks in the curve of his palms. Waves of wanting washed over them both. He wrapped his arms tightly around her and held her, rocking her gently in his arms. "Tell me, Jen Pearl", he said again.

She shook her head vehemently. "I can't do that, Horace Burton. You know how I feel, but as long as I'm married to Otis I can't say it to you or nobody else. Now please, if you love me, let me go. Please, don't do this to me any more. This hurts me way too much for words. It hurts so much I can't breathe for days after you're gone. I don't want to hurt no more, Horace."

A low sob eased past the man's lips as he kissed her one last time. He clung to her and she to him as he whispered into her ear. "I'll never love another woman the way I love you, Jen Pearl." And then he was gone, disappearing out the door and down the road.

Jen Pearl felt her body tense, her muscles bristling as her spine pulled taut. She stretched the length of her legs out in front of her, rubbing at the line of broken blood vessels that left an unsightly trail out from her knees, up her thighs and down her calves. She could feel Angelette staring at her, waiting for her to respond, and so she did.

"We didn't for the same reasons you and Tate did," she finally answered, her gaze meeting Angelette's.

Silence filled the space between them, rising thick like the mist out over the ocean. Angelette lay back against the wet sand, wrapping her arms around her torso. Although the air was still warm, a chill crawled up the length of her spine. Miss Jen Pearl lay back beside her and the two women stared up toward the sky, watching the onset of the storm rolling in above them.

Tate had stood nervously as she'd locked the door behind them. His hands had been pushed deep into his pockets, his fingers scratching against the line of his leg. Angelette could feel him staring at her, his eyes dancing over the white tee shirt she wore. The garment hung like a dress, the hem falling to her knees. Her well-toned calves and manicured toes peeked from beneath. Tate could see that she was naked beneath the white cotton and the thought caused a wave of heat to rush from one end of his body to the other. Drawing a deep breath, he felt his nails dig into his upper thigh and he bit down hard against his bottom lip.

Angelette smiled sweetly, nodding her head in his direction. "You want something to eat or drink?" she asked, moving to the refrigerator. She pulled open the door and leaned to peer inside. "I've got Kool-Aid, apple juice, and some beer."

Tate shook his head. "No, thanks."

Angelette closed the refrigerator door and made her way back to Tate's side. "Why are you shaking, Tate?" she asked, looking at him anxiously.

The man shrugged his broad shoulders, trying not to stare at her. He didn't want to look at her, didn't want her to see the yearning that consumed his expression. He could feel the heat rising off her body, clouding the space between them as it tangled thick and full with his own rising ardor. Perspiration beaded against Tate's brow and he swiped his hand across his face.

"I really should be going, Angelette. I just wanted to check that you were okay," he said, taking a step back and moving to the other side of the worn sofa.

Angelette nodded her head slowly. "I'm fine. Just a little lonely I guess. I'm just tired of being here all by myself. Again," she whispered softly.

She knew that Tate understood. Each and every time Graye got himself thrown in jail, Tate would be the one to come and tell her, to check that she was well, offering his services if ever they were needed. Since that first day they had met, the two had become fast friends, sharing time and space easily.

Over the years, Tate had finished medical school, forgoing a medical practice to do research for a large pharmaceutical corporation. He had been married, then had divorced the woman he claimed hadn't been right for him from the get go. They'd had one child, a little girl who Tate loved with all his heart. He was a good father, loving and attentive, embracing the responsibilities of parenthood whole-heartedly. Angelette enjoyed hearing about his accomplishments, pride gleaning from her eyes with each of his successes.

Tate tried to change the subject, to calm the wave of emotions that seemed to be demanding attention around them. "Did you send in that application I left for you?" he asked.

Angelette grinned, her head bobbing up and down against her shoulders. "I did. I mailed it last week. Do you really think I can get in?"

"Why not? Tate responded, nodding with her. "You can do anything you set your mind to, Angelette." For ten full minutes he extolled her virtues, inflating her fragile ego with hope and promise of what she could do and be and accomplish if she were so inclined. He was supportive and caring and as he made her feel special, Angelette could feel the tears rising to her eyes and clouding her vision.

Tate's gaze met hers, the sight of her crying causing him to pause. He suddenly had an intense need to hold her, to comfort her, to wipe away the moisture that slid with ease down her cheeks. There was something that lingered in her stare, something he couldn't read and suddenly he realized that he didn't want to, believing his ignorance would indeed be bliss. She was still staring at him intently, her gaze unwavering, and then she moved again, circling the couch to stand back at his side. Angelette reached out and took his hand in hers, her fingers entwining with his as she pressed her palm to his palm.

"I really should be going, Angelette. I don't think it's a good idea for me to be here right now," he said, his voice a loud whisper that seemed to rise from out of his chest and dissipate before he could get the sound past his lips good. His tone sounded strange, even to him, reverberating harshly in his own ears.

Angelette simply smiled again and Tate marveled at the lush lips that pulled easily over the line of her brilliant white teeth. He suddenly imagined himself kissing those lips, drawing first her bottom lip between his own and then her top as his tongue danced inside the warm cavity of her mouth. An erection stiffened in his pants, pushing anxiously against the front of his slacks.

"You know you don't have anywhere else to go, Tate," Angelette said, stepping in even closer. Tate could smell the scent of Ivory soap that kissed her skin, her flesh still heated from the bath she'd soaked in. He pressed his eyes closed for a quick minute, flooding his lungs with oxygen and he struggled to maintain control. When he opened them, she was still staring at him intently, wanting oozing past her long lashes. One last tear had puddled at the edge of her eye and before it could fall Angelette wiped it away with her index finger.

Without thinking, Tate moved against her, closing what little space lay between them. He dropped a palm to her waist and eased her against his body pressing the length of himself into her pelvis. He felt her shudder, her body quivering ever so slightly beneath his touch. Neither of them said a word as Angelette pressed her palms into his chest, her fingers caressing the fabric of his silk shirt. Tate leaned as if to kiss her lips, hesitating before his mouth met hers. He suddenly sighed, moving to brush his cheek against her cheek, the warmth of his breath blowing past her earlobe. Wrapping his arms around her he hugged her tightly.

Angelette had never before felt so safe. She fit inside the curve of Tate's embrace as if it had been made especially for her. She could feel his heart beating against her breast, beating in sync with her own heartbeat. She could feel herself falling into his hold, yearning for the beauty of his touch and she wanted to open herself to him, spreading herself whole for him to know and discover. They both inhaled at the same time, sharing the air between them.

Tate pressed his lips to her cheek, his mouth lingering against her flesh for a quick moment, then he whispered into her ear. "Graye's my friend, Angelette. And he trusts me," he said softly.

Angelette could feel the wet warmth of his tears falling against her cheek. "Graye ain't your friend, Tate. Graye don't care nothing about you," she whispered back "Graye don't care about nobody but Graye."

Tate tightened his grip around her torso, stifling a sob that had caught in his chest. His fingers danced with ease down her back, stopping at the rise of her buttocks. His hands moved to grip her shoulders as he stepped back a second time. The heat that had risen between them was stifling. Tate laughed to ease the sudden tension, an uneasy cacophony that resonated through the room like fingernails on a chalkboard. Angelette pressed two fingers to his lips to silence him.

He pressed his palm to her face, allowing his fingers to lightly trace the line of her profile. Angelette continued to stare into his eyes, bewitched by the sadness that seeped past his lashes. She felt helpless, the depths of his anguish, and her own, filling her with grief.

"This isn't right, Angelette," the man gasped. "You know this isn't right."

She shook her head. "There ain't much in my life that has ever been right, Tate. But you and I both know this is different. What's between us has always been different. You've been feeling it just like I been feeling it. That's why you came here tonight, why you keep coming. But it scares you. It scares you just like it scares me." Angelette paused, her stare flickering back and forth over his before she continued. "If anything has ever been right, Tate, then it's me loving you and you loving me back. 'Cause you know I love you. I've never said it before, but you can feel it. You know it like I know it. I love you," she whispered, tears once again streaming down her face.

The man heaved a deep sigh, falling deeper into the moment. He knew he needed to leave, to run from her and this place as fast as he could run, but his legs were planted where he stood, holding him hostage in this space that was her space and Graye's space. Love holding him hostage and refusing to let him go. He shook his head, the appendage suddenly heavy against his thick neck. "Yes, I do," he whispered back. "I do love you, Angelette. I love you so much that it hurts."

Angelette moved back against him, her mouth falling to the spot beneath his chin, her tongue dancing warm and wet against his flesh. "Do you want me, Tate?" she whispered into his flesh, wet kisses punctuating her question. "Please, say you want me," she implored.

Tate could feel his head nodding, his body reacting on its own accord, oblivious to what reason was trying to tell it. Tate was suddenly aware of every rising hair, every muscle and tendon and blood vessel that throbbed beneath his skin. Wanting her didn't begin to express what he was feeling. A twinge of raw adrenaline slid through his chest. His insides shuddered violently and he swallowed hard, licking his lips slowly.

Angelette leaned up on her toes and pressed her mouth to his mouth. Tate kissed her back, a soft feathery touch of his flesh against hers. Parting his lips he stroked her softness with the tip of his tongue and to his delight, Angelette opened her mouth to him, her lips parting easily. Their tongues touched tentatively then began a slow, easy caress in the warm cavity. Tate groaned his approval. She was exquisitely sweet, and he felt his breath being sucked from his soul.

Dropping down against the sofa, Tate lifted her so that she lay on top of him, her body melting easily into his. All caution and pretense was now totally gone, concerns and thoughts of Graye forgotten. Boldly, Tate slipped his hands beneath her tee shirt. His palms danced across her bare breasts and her nipples suddenly hardened unbearably as he pulled first at one and then the other. His hands dropped and circled around her waist. He caressed the smooth slopes and hollows of her back, his fingers fondling her flesh lightly as he slowly explored every inch of her. His palms glided downwards, across the small of her back to the sleek, slanting slope of her hips and then he cradled the firm softness of her buttocks beneath his palms. Tracing his fingers down the soft, dividing rift, he reached the tops of her thighs, his fingertips quivering with anticipation.

Flipping her against the back of the sofa, Tate pressed himself against her. His kisses intensified, hunger rising in intensity. With his confidence completely returned, he pressed his hand between her legs, his fingers searching out the slick, moist heat. Angelette moaned with pleasure as her thighs edged apart. Tate lifted her leg, dropping it over the back of the couch. Waves of current coursed through her pelvis as Tate began to stroke the softness between her thighs. He moved with long, penetrating caresses, circling, probing, stroking faster until his hand became a blur and then, quite abruptly, with a loud cry, Angelette climaxed. A long groan of satisfaction escaped her clenched teeth as her body shuddered in sheer ecstasy. Her leg dropped as her thighs firmly locked together, imprisoning his buried fingers. Angelette struggled to breathe, gasping for air.

Tate shifted his body and pulled the cotton shirt up and over her head. He stared down at her nakedness, his gaze wafting with appreciation. He had not seen beauty before seeing her beauty. She was divine. Skin like bronzed satin, the lush lines and curves of her body a sculptor's delight. He stared, allowing the vision of her to be burned forever into his memory.

With every ounce of energy that she possessed Angelette pulled at his clothes, popping the line of buttons that closed his shirt. Lifting his hips, he let her ease his pants past his buttocks and to the floor, fabric puddling at his feet. He was glorious, solid muscle beneath dark chocolate flesh. Every inch of him was hard and wanting. Angelette pushed him back against the sofa, positioning herself above him as she searched out his mouth and kissed him intently. Her skin burned hot against his, perspiration simmering against his flesh.

Reaching for her breasts, Tate cradled them against his cheek, then leaned to suckling one nipple and then the other. As Angelette straddled him, the slick moisture of her desire painted his abdomen and thighs. Angelette could feel the hard length of him graze the sensitive flesh inside her leg. She whispered his name over and over, her mouth trailing kisses across his face, down his neck and over his chest.

Tate grabbed his manhood and he held it upright with one hand as he lowered Angelette by the waist onto it slowly with his other hand. Angelette cried out with pleasure, her fists clenched on either side of Tate's shoulders. The length of her dark hair cascaded down over her face, brushing along his torso.

"Oh, sweet Jesus," Tate cried as he pulled himself out of her and slowly pushed himself back in.

Lifting herself up and down, Angelette rode him slowly, her head dropping back against her neck. Tate reveled in the moment, overcome by the wealth of sensations that had consumed him. His hands danced over her torso, caressing her breasts, stroking the line of her throat. His fingers tickled her flesh, drawing circles over the slightly protruding belly button and lines down to the door of her secret treasure. Fire swelled out of control between them.

Sitting up, Tate pulled her tight against him, stalling her movements. He held her close, panting heavily into her ear as Angelette hugged him back. Breaking the intimate connection, Tate rolled her against the sofa, easing her over the arm of the structure.

"Bend over for me, baby," he whispered, barely managing the words. He was so close to the edge he could barely hold on.

Angelette did as she was asked, rolling onto her belly, her legs spread wide, as Tate slid a pillow beneath her abdomen. He toyed with her femininity, sliding the head of his manhood up and down against her. Angelette strained against him, wanting to feel him back inside her, but Tate wouldn't allow it. She whimpered and buried her face against the arm of the couch as his fingers danced teasingly between her legs. She lifted her hips upward, imploring him to enter her, and then Tate thrust the length of himself forward, entering her easily.

Angelette screamed. "Oh God! Yes, baby. Yes!"

Tate shoved himself in and ripped himself out just to push back in again. His gestures were quick and frantic, delirious with hunger. Angelette braced herself on her hands and knees, her legs spread wide, one knee clinging to the edge of the sofa. She met his thrusts with equal force, screaming and calling his name over and over again. The room spun, the walls circling faster and faster around them and then Tate pulled himself from her again, easing her onto her back. He hovered above her, his gaze locked with hers. The look was consuming, emotion spilling past his lashes, and hers. As he entered her again, his eyes widened, his stare more intense. Angelette could feel herself drowning in the depths of it, every wish and dream and want between them, shimmering against his cornea. He held her tightly, his body melding deeply into hers and then he fell down against her, allowing her to catch all of his weight as he spooned his warm body around hers, every muscle quivering with intensity. They both fell into the realms of an earth-shattering orgasm. Tate filled the wealth of her, his love seeping deep into the hollow chasm of her private garden where it watered her spirit, nurturing her back to life.

Angelette had fallen to sleep with Tate lying above her, his weight shielding and protective around her. When she awoke, Tate was gone, his kisses still burning against her flesh. Days later he was dead and she had wished that she had been. Instead, here she was, left alone, haunted by the memory of everything they'd shared and the price they'd paid for believing it would last them a lifetime. She had loved Tate and he had returned her love with all he'd had to give. Then Graye had taken it all away. Angelette swiped angrily at the tears that seeped from her eyes, brushing sand across her face.

Miss Jen Pearl was leaning up on her elbows, staring as Angelette shook the memories from her mind. The old woman shook her head as her gaze locked with Angelette's. She continued talking. "You let Tate touch your heart and that cut Graye deeper than when you let Tate have your body. I know. I know because I saw how much my Otis bled each and every time he looked me in the eyes and saw me wanting Doc Burton. I could see his hurt when he wanted it to be just him and me and Doc was somewhere in the room with us because he was always there in my heart."

She paused, her voice dropping to a loud whisper. "There are all kinds of affairs, Angelette. But I imagine our kind was the worst kind," she muttered softly. "It was the worst kind because even though we didn't mean for it to happen, it did. And it was bigger than we knew how to control and so we let it control us. Got so good to us it made us crazy and when we was crazy, we couldn't be whole for Otis and Graye. And they didn't know how to be whole for themselves.

"Tate had your heart. Doc had mine. Ain't no man alive who can fight a ghost like that. No man.

Graye keep trying but even with Tate dead he know he can never have that part of you that Tate had." Miss Jen Pearl heaved a deep sigh. Her voice dropped, concern and dread in her tone. "And Graye being the man he is, he won't ever accept that and he won't let you go."

Angelette sat with her eyes closed tight, refusing to meet the woman's gaze. The truth was cutting, sweeping through her spirit with a vengeance. Above them, thunder clapped across the darkened sky, the roar of noise wafting hand and hand with the dark clouds that had rolled in above them.

"So what do I do now?" Angelette finally asked.

Miss Jen Pearl came to her feet, extending her hand to Angelette as the sky suddenly opened with full force, torrential rains gushing down suddenly. "Only you can answer that, child. But whatever you decide, it has to be your choice. No one else's. This is your life, Baby Doll. You decide how you want to live it."

TWENTY-FOUR

Graye had spent most of the morning going from one home to another in search of the two women. No one, not his sisters nor his brothers would tell him where Angelette and Miss Jen Pearl had gone off to hide. Everyone claiming that they didn't know a thing.

As he made his way back home, Graye's frustration was beginning to show on his face. Deep lines creased his forehead and his jaw hurt from clenching his teeth so tightly. His cheeks were flush with color, a deep, burgandy red raging deep in the hollow dimples that pitted his flesh. His nails had dug imprints into his palms from clenching his hands so tightly and thus far he had only thrown one punch, his fist shattering a mirror in that old white man's office. And still he had no answers. No idea where that bitch had absconded to, taking his mother away from him.

He walked a tight circle in the center of his living room. The muscles had tightened across his abdomen, anxiety knotting in the pit of stomach. Bile rose from his midsection, filling his mouth and he spat venom to the floor. Rage spewed from his pores and every muscle in his body was racked with pain. He would not have believed it remotely possible to hurt so much, but he hurt. Pain crippled his emotions.

His heart felt as if it had been splintered into brittle, jagged shards, nothing neat or clean about the break. Every fiber of his being felt disjointed, disconnected, longing for relief that didn't feel possible. Angelette was gone and he couldn't understand why she had left him. Why wasn't she here to make it all better, to calm the unrest that was threatening to consume him? She had promised him forever, and he had trusted her. Then she'd betrayed him and now she needed to pay for all his hurt. She need to pay because no man would allow his heart and his home to be breached without seeking retribution. His father had taught him that. He'd learned the lessons and he'd lived by them. It was what he was supposed to do. Graye wiped his palm across his eyes, tears dampening his flesh as moisture trickled across the length of his fingers.

"Don't you dare cry," Otis McAdams commanded, the back of his hand connecting to the woman's face. "Cry and see if I don't give you something to cry for."

Miss Jen Pearl dropped to the floor, the hardwood rushing to meet her. She cradled her bruised flesh with her fingers, heaving a deep sigh as she struggled to stifle her tears.

"Why you do that, Otis? You ain't had no cause to hit me like that," she sputtered, as he hovered threateningly above her.

Otis shook his head, rage tattooed on his face. "You sleep with that white man?" he asked, his words coated in venom. "Did you let him touch you?"

"No," Jen Pearl shouted back, shaking her head vehemently. "You know I wouldn't do nothing like that. I love you, Otis. Only you!"

Otis stepped back and heaved a deep sigh, his hands still clenched into tight fists at his sides. In the corner of the room, five-year old Graye stood wide-eyed, his thumb pulled into his mouth, tears draining down over his chubby cheeks. He met his mother's concerned gaze, his own pale gray eyes the size of large saucers in his small face.

"Graye, it's okay, baby," Miss Jen Pearl said softly. "It's okay, baby boy. Daddy ain't mad, honey. Mama just slipped. Everything's going to be just fine," she said, her gaze racing from the child to his father and back again.

Graye stood shaking where he stood, his bowed legs quivering with fear. Moisture suddenly flooded the seat of his britches as he soiled his denim pants, piss running the length of his short legs and puddling against the floors beneath his bare feet. He glanced down, holding his breath with dread as the acrid scent of warm urine filled the room. He cried harder, embarrassed, and ashamed, and fearful that his predicament would further incite his father's rage. He looked back toward his parents. His father never looked in his direction. His mother tried to smile, her hand still pressed to her face as she shook her head from side to side. "It's okay, baby boy. Mama loves you," she said. "Everything's going to be just fine."

Otis snarled, leveraging his foot to give the woman a swift kick to her abdomen. He stood staring down at her as she doubled over in pain. "I'll kill him dead before I let him have you, Jen Pearl. I swear, I'll kill him dead and it'll be all your fault," he swore, profanity punctuating his statement.'

Spinning toward the door, Otis looked in his son's direction for the first time. He stood staring at the child as his breathing finally eased up, the tightened muscles slowly relaxing. He nodded his head and smiled, a wide grin suddenly filling his face. He extended a hand in the little boy's direction and called out to the child who was eyeing him warily. "Daddy didn't mean to scare his baby. Come on, son. Come on with your daddy. You're daddy's little man, ain't you?"

As she lay curled on the floor, hurt racking every inch of her petite frame, Jen Pearl gestured for her son to do as he was told. "Go on, Graye," she sobbed. "Go on and be a good boy for your daddy," she said softly. And he did, stepping over his mother's bruised body as his father led him out the room.

Graye pulled the half-full bottle to his lips and took another drink of the bitter fluid. Jack Daniel's filled his mouth, rushing down the back of his throat as he swallowed. He took a fourth and fifth swig, swiping the back of his free hand across his mouth. His other hand tightened around the neck of the amber-colored glass as he paced the short length of carpeted floor.

The drink had always been able to ease his hurt. To soothe him. But it was taking more and more of it to calm his nerves this day. He had to find them. Had to know where she was. He had to know why. Why didn't she love him? Why didn't she want him? Why had she loved Tate more?

Everybody had loved Tate. Tate's good-hearted nature had drawn people in and had held them tight to him. Tate had been special. Graye couldn't help reflecting back on the man who had claimed him as his best friend. Tate had opened his heart to Graye and had welcomed him in without hesitation. Tate had stood by his side and had defended him, even when Graye had been at his worse. Then Tate had done what no man should have ever done. He had stolen what wasn't his to have. He had taken what should have belonged only to Graye.

Tate stood in wait outside the large, prison facility. Graye caught sight of him first, stopping in his tracks as he eyed the man with an obvious sneer. There was just a hint of chill in the early morning air, the last glazing of a late night frost beginning to dissipate beneath the rising sunshine. Tate stood with his back facing the prison's heavy metal gate, the man's gaze searching the skyline out in the distance. He wore a brown leather bomber's jacket, denim jeans, and steel-toed boots, the casual attire seemingly out of place on his lean frame.

As if sensing Graye's stare boring a hole straight through him, Tate turned an about face, the two men meeting each other's eyes evenly. Tate nodded in greeting, his facial muscles barely quivering with acknowledgement. He pushed his hands deep into his pockets. A prison guard tapped Graye on his shoulder, motioning toward freedom with a quick wave of his hand. Graye began to walk again, moving slowly in the direction the man had pointed.

As he made his way to Tate's side the man turned, walking along beside him as they sauntered toward Tate's car. Behind them the loud clank of the prison gate closing resounded through the air. Neither man was moved by the harsh clamor of iron striking iron, both having heard it too many times before to be roused. No one spoke as they eased up to the car. Tate unlocked the trunk then moved to the driver's side door and slid behind the steering wheel. He waited as Graye dropped the brown paper bag filled with his personal possessions into the rear cavity, slamming the lid closed. After the man was seated beside him, Tate started the engine, pulled the vehicle past the rifle-toting guards standing watch at the entrance and eased into the first signs of traffic that signaled the beginning of a new day.

Graye didn't recognize the song on the radio, a nondescript medley of strings and woodwinds blowing too softly from the speakers. He reached for the radio and pushed the seek button, flipping through the stations until he found Gwen Stefani calling for her girl to holla back. The bass was heavy and vibrated through the small vehicle, the Toyota Camry shaking in time with the music as he turned up the volume. Both men were grateful for the noise that served as a distraction.

"So what you come for?" Graye finally asked.

"You needed a ride, didn't you?"

"I could have caught the bus."

"You could have but Angelette didn't want you to have to do that. She asked me to pick you up."

Graye cut his eye toward the man. "You've seen Angelette?"

"She called me. I haven't seen her."

"Uh huh."

Tate shrugged. "Everyone's getting ready for your mama's birthday party. I'm sure Miss Jen Pearl's going to be glad to have you home."

Graye didn't bother to respond. Silence filled the small space, clouding the air.

Tate cleared his throat, tightening his grip on the steering wheel. There was something on his mind and Graye could feel it, knowing Tate well. "What's on your mind, Tate?" he finally asked, shifting in his seat to face the man.

Tate moistened his lips, his thick tongue rolling over the surface. Then he spoke. "Been thinking a lot about what you said before, Graye. What you said about me and Angelette."

"Yeah."

"I done took a lot of shit from you over the years 'cause you were my friend. But I ain't taking no more, Graye. Done had enough. Done had enough of you and all of your mess and I'm through. We ain't friends. We ain't never gone be friends 'cause you don't know what that means and neither do I anymore. I just know I can do better. I can do better than you."

"What you mean?"

"Just what I said. I'm here now 'cause Angelette asked me to be here. I don't know why and I don't much care. But like I told her and like I'm telling you, this is the last time."

Graye grinned. "Whatever."

Tate nodded his head slowly. "Yeah, whatever."

Neither spoke again until Tate pulled into the driveway of Graye's home. Both stared toward the front door as Angelette pulled it open, standing in the entrance way staring at the two of them.

Tate chuckled softly under his breath. "You don't deserve her, Graye. And you know it," he said, the words falling before he could stop them from spilling out of his thoughts.

"Maybe. Maybe not. But she's mine."

Tate laughed out loud, turning to stare the man in his eye. "You think so. But we both know the truth, don't we Graye. We both know she will never be yours. Not all of her. Not what matters most."

Graye bristled. "She's mine," he stated emphatically, his voice rising harshly.

The other man nodded. "Go on inside, Graye. Have a good life."

Graye clenched a heavy fist against his leg. He gestured as if he wanted to swing. Tate didn't flinch, his eyes locked on Graye's face.

"Take your best shot, Graye. I promise you it'll be your last."

"You sure about that?"

"You better believe it, brother. Just like we both know who your girl is going to be thinking about when you close that door."

"We know she won't be thinking about your ass."

Tate grinned, his eyes narrowing ever so slightly. "Take what you can get, Graye. Sloppy seconds is better than nothing."

"Fuck you."

"No, son. Fuck you." Tate reached in front of Graye and pushed the door open. "Fuck you, Graye."

As Graye eased his way out, Tate's last words rang harshly in his ears, knowing that they both knew who Angelette would be thinking about and it wouldn't be Graye that she had on her mind. As he made his way to his front door, Tate pulling out of the driveway behind him, Graye could already see it in her eyes.

Graye gulped the last of the bitter fluid then dropped the empty liquor bottle to the floor. He stepped out on the front porch and stared over to his mother's house. Although the pale flicker of a nightlight shone through the partially drawn shades in the front window he knew she wasn't home. His mother was lost somewhere, spirited away by Angelette.

High above him the full moon shimmered brightly in the dark sky. Graye inhaled the damp air into his lungs, sucking in deep breaths like a drowning man pulled safe from a watery death. They had predicted rain and there was just the faintest hint of it floating through the atmosphere.

He and Tate had often played in the rain, dodging through the fields as the clouds wept above their heads. Life had been sweet then, happiness easy to find and easier to share. It had been as if their laughter had been captured in the drops of spray, swirling over the dark earth and down to the ground, joy and moisture watering life around them.

They heard the screams coming from the house, Miss Jen Pearl crying out, her tone pleading. Graye stopped, his spidery legs frozen in place, his eyes searching through the darkness toward the front door for his mother and any hint or sign that would let him know all would soon be well. Tate stood by his side. His friend rested a heavy hand on his shoulder and Graye shrugged it off, moving a step closer toward the commotion that had captured their attention. A moment later, Tate was right back at his side, his hand back on Graye's shoulder. Inside the house, his father's deep voice bellowed vile enumerations, calling his mother names no man should have ever called any woman.

"It's going to be okay," Tate said softly. "My folks, they fight too," he whispered, the cool night air carrying his words up into the dark sky.

Graye turned to look at his friend. "It just ain't right," he whispered back. "It just ain't right."

"I know," Tate answered, "but your father doesn't mean it. I'm sure he doesn't."

Gray shook his head. "No, you don't understand. It ain't right for nobody to be taken nothing that belongs to me and my daddy. It just ain't right."

Tate looked at him curiously.

"I should go bust that cracker in his head."

"Who?"

"Doc Burton. My daddy hates that man. Says he tryin' to take my mama away from us. I should go bust his head good."

Tate's bottom lip dropped down toward his chin, an incredulous expression crossing his face. "Doctor Burton? That can't be..."

Graye nodded his head, the appendage bouncing like a loose ball bearing against his shoulders. "My daddy'll fix him. He'll fix him good. Don't nobody take what belongs to us. Nobody," he spat, venom spinning the words out of his mouth.

Silence had replaced the noise. The two boys stood still, their gazes still locked on the front door. A few minutes felt like an eternity and then Miss Jen Pearl appeared on the front porch, calling out to them in her usual calm and even tone.

"Graye! Tate! What you boys doing out here in this weather? Come on inside. Your daddy done made you two some popcorn and I've got hot chocolate on the stove. You two gone catch pneumonia playing out here in the rain."

His friend Tate slapped him easily across the back, a wide grin shimmering beneath the faintest hint of moonlight. "Things will be different now. You wait and see. Things can change."

Graye smiled at the memory. Maybe he would still bust old Doc Burton in his head, he thought, the booze egging him on to do something, anything. Maybe he would do that for his daddy since his daddy never got the chance to do it for himself.

As Graye moved to step off the porch he tripped over his own feet, falling down the short length of steps to the ground below. He landed against the damp grass with a harsh bang, his foot catching in a row of plastic plants. He cursed loudly, the odious tone of his voice filtering through the silent air. Pulling his legs out straight in front of him, he eased his buttocks onto the bottom step and leaned back against the length of risers and treads. His head hurt and now his body ached even more from where it had slammed into the dry earth. Tears suddenly filled his bloodshot eyes and then he heard his name being called from somewhere above him, a familiar voice reminding him that things could indeed be different.

Miss Jen Pearl lay sprawled across the twin bed. The motel room was old and small but clean, sufficient enough for her and Angelette to get a good night's sleep. On the other side of the bathroom door, Angelette was soaking in a tub of lilac-scented bath bubbles and hot water, singing along at the top of her lungs with a small transistor radio she'd propped against the closed toilet seat.

Miss Jen Pearl just shook her head at the commotion, sending a silent prayer of thanks for any diversion that could bring the younger woman a minute of happiness. Miss Jen Pearl heaved a deep sigh, blowing a gust of warm breath past her lips. There was so much of her in Angelette that she felt as if someone had held up a mirror to her soul the day the girl had come into their lives. She was determined though that Angelette would learn something from her mistakes and perhaps have the opportunity to do what she hadn't been able to do for herself.

She shook her head against the pillow. Her choices hadn't always been good choices but they'd been necessary. They'd been necessary at the time, she thought, and that had to be reason enough to not let the bad times outweigh the good. That's why she'd worked so hard to bury the bad memories with Otis, closing the casket lid on his dead body and all that unhappiness at the same time.

Miss Jen Pearl heaved a deep sigh. Rolling onto her stomach, she began to hum along with Angelette and the radio. The local college station was spinning oldies, paying homage to Sam Cooke. Sam was oozing about change that was gonna come, the words seeping out of his soul like clover honey. The old woman smiled as Angelette's voice came floating louder into the room, crying about it being too hard living, but clinging to the promise of that change coming. Minutes later, Sam and Angelette came out of the bathroom shaking like a bowl of jello, the young girl sashaying in black boy-cut panties and a red silk brassiere. Her hands skated across her hips, her backbone slipping as she shook every square inch of her body. Miss Jen Pearl laughed as Angelette danced around the room, then without a thought climbed up on the twin bed to *Cha-Cha-Cha* in her own white, polyester slip and cotton undergarments. The duo finally fell back against their respective mattresses contemplating just how wonderful a world it really could be, Sam's soothing tone lulling them both into a state of comfort.

As the night disc jockey whispered the station's calls sign over the airwaves, Angelette leaned up on her elbows, her gaze meeting Miss Jen Pearl's. They stared, their silent conversation mediated by a higher power, then both lay back across their beds to succumb to a good night's sleep. Though neither of them had spoken the words aloud, both knew the moment couldn't last. There could truly be no running from those things they needed to face head on. Both knew what needed to be done. Tomorrow, they would be heading back home.

TWENTY-FIVE

Even as they'd dressed, repacked their belongings and had made their way back to the bus station neither woman had anything to say. The silence between them was almost deafening as it filled the space around them. The bus ride was equally as quiet as both women sat lost in thought, imagining what might be waiting for them when they returned home.

Miss Jen Pearl hadn't thought much about Otis since she and Angelette had last spoken, but she'd given much consideration to Graye. She blamed herself for her son's many transgressions, imagining that she should have done more to contain her child's wretched behavior. She had tried in earnest to do right by the boy, treating him no different from how she'd treated her other children. But hindsight was twenty-twenty and Miss Jen Pearl imagined that she should have done more for Graye because Graye had surely needed more from her.

Graye had been all kinds of bad as a youngster, one of those children other folks hated to see coming. There had been no controlling him, most especially when Graye was hell bent on causing any kind of a commotion. Otis had encouraged the behavior and despite her best efforts, Otis had managed to gain more influence over Graye than she had.

He'd barely been in his teens when he'd started to abuse drugs and alcohol, not giving a thought to sipping whiskey from his daddy's stash or buying them funny cigarettes from them boys that spent their time blending into the landscape down on the local corners. Miss Jen Pearl had heard the many rumors that had Graye selling crack and cocaine down at the club but he'd insisted they were all lies the few times she'd questioned him, threatening to turn him right over to the law.

As Graye had reached adulthood, Miss Jen Pearl acknowledged turning a blind eye and deaf ear to much of his behavior, but she'd grown weary with the constant battles that continually disrupted what little peace she could muster to find in her own home. And somewhere along the way she had failed her son. Had failed him miserably and now everyone else was suffering for that sin. Miss Jen Pearl heaved a deep sigh, swiping at her eyes with the back of her hands. Her eyes were dry, but her heart was heavy, hurt swelling it beyond capacity. Anxiety plagued her, cramping her intestines and Miss Jen Pearl suddenly felt as if she might be ill.

As if sensing her discomfort, Angelette leaned her head on Miss Jen Pearl's shoulder and reached for her hands, caressing the woman's arthritic fingers with the palm of her hand. Miss Jen Pearl nodded ever so slightly, then focused her attention to the landscape sweeping past them outside, watching as home rolled quickly in their direction.

Miss Jen Pearl had sprung for a taxicab to transport them from the bus station to home. She could have easily called Doc Burton or one of her children, but neither she nor Angelette had been ready to be bothered with any of them. The twelve-dollar expenditure to carry them less than five miles home had been well worth the cost.

As the old yellow Chevy, with its dented taxi sign perched askew on the car's rooftop, eased into the driveway of their family home, the two women caught sight of Graye, both eyeing him at the same time. They saw him before he even noticed the taxi make its turn onto the old gravel road. He was sitting at the top of Miss Jen Pearl's front steps, his head resting in the palms of his hands. His torso was hunched over his thighs, leaning forward as if his body was too heavy for his legs to carry. A throng of empty beer cans and two empty scotch bottles lay strewn around the yard below his feet, the tide of litter sullying the plastic gardens planted below the stoop.

Both women braced themselves for an onslaught of emotion, expecting a battalion of hostility and rank anger to greet them, but when Graye looked up, his gaze meeting his mother's first and then his wife's, he was unusually calm. He stared at them both as if seeing them for the very first time and then he smiled.

If she had to label what she saw behind his pale eyes she would have named it joy, Miss Jen Pearl thought for just a brief moment. It seemed to paint her son's expression with an abundance of light and laughter, building in momentum as it spread up and out of his body. Graye jumped to his feet, hysterical with laughter as he swept Angelette up into his arms and swung her around in a tight circle. He grinned foolishly as he glanced in his mother's direction and in that moment, Miss Jen Pearl was happy to laugh with him.

"Good morning, Graye. How you doin', baby boy?"

"I'm good, Mama. Glad you home." He kissed Angelette, his mouth moving against hers with a sudden urgency. "I knew you'd come back," he whispered into her hair, his fingers pulling through the length of black silk. "Just knew it."

Angelette said nothing, maneuvering out of Graye's grip as she followed Miss Jen Pearl up the steps and in through the front door. Graye was right on their heels as they moved inside. Nana Leah sat room center, turning to stare as they came into the home.

"Hey, Mama. You doin' okay?" Miss Jen Pearl asked as she leaned to kiss the matriarch's forehead.

The old woman grunted. "Just fine. Where you been?"

The other woman just shrugged. "We just needed some time away. Just needed to disappear for a quick minute."

Nana Leah held her gaze, her eyes skipping back and forth across her daughter's face. The two said nothing, both staring intently at the other and then Nana Leah grunted for a second time, the obnoxious noise ringing loudly through the small room.

Graye laughed, dropping down onto the living room sofa. "I'm wit' Nana," he exclaimed. "That was one long minute!"

Miss Jen Pearl shook her head, changing the subject. "Have them girls been here to make sure you've been taking your medication, Mama?"

"'Dem girls been in the way. That's all they been. Been bossy and nosey. Got right on my nerves."

"Then I'm glad to hear things went well."

Nana Leah sucked her teeth. "Tch! You should have been here taking care of yo' business. Running 'round like you ain't had no responsibilities."

Miss Jen Pearl rolled her eyes, her gaze meeting Angelette's for a quick second. The young woman had not moved from the edge of the wing back chair she'd taken a seat in. She sat as though ready to run, nervous energy making her quiver in her seat. Across the room, Graye continued to watch the woman, afraid that if he took his eyes off her for only a second she might disappear from his sight again. Miss Jen Pearl couldn't help but think that things had gone back to normal quicker than either she or Angelette had been ready for them. And yet, in some way, somehow, everything seemed to have taken a turn and changed.

Peering out her front window, Miss Jen Pearl shook her head. "Graye, you make that mess out in my yard?"

The man shrugged, his broad shoulders pushing toward his ears.

Miss Jen Pearl cut her eye in his direction, her head still waving from side to side. "Make sure you pick up all that trash. You know good and well I don't let my yard look like that. All them bottles all over the place like that. Humph!"

"Yes, ma'am," Graye responded. "I'll take care of it."

"Yes, you will," she muttered, brushing at the length of sheer fabric that curtained her window.

Graye grinned, winking an eye at his grandmother who was shaking a wrinkled finger in his direction. Reaching into his back pocket he pulled a small flask into his hand, unscrewed the cap, and took a quick sip of its contents. As he did his mother eyed him with annoyance, her arms crossing over her chest as she tapped her toe against the hardwood floor.

"Ain't it a little early for that?" Miss Jen Pearl asked.

Graye shrugged a second time, then took another sip before recapping the container and slipping it back into its hiding spot. "Man needs a little joy juice every now and then," he answered, a wide grin filling his face.

His mother stood staring at him, suddenly reminded of all the times Otis had laid claim to needing him some joy juice. "You need to get you some help with that drinking problem, Graye," she said, moving to stand in front of him.

"I ain't got no drinking problem," Graye chuckled. "I ain't got no problems drinking at all."

Nana Leah snorted loudly, the gesture causing them all to turn to stare in her direction. "You needs to leave that boy be," the old woman professed, dismissing them with a wave of her hand. "A man can't have you fussing at him all the time," she said.

Miss Jen Pearl rolled her eyes skyward and the older woman continued.

"Graye?"

"Yes, Nana?"

"Go clean that yard up and take your mess back across the street. I'm tired of seeing you."

Graye laughed. "Yes, ma'am," he said, rising to his feet. "Me and Angelette goin' home right now!"

Jackson Pratt's sixteen-year old sister had been the first female Graye had seen completely naked. He'd only been fourteen years old at the time. A fourteen-year-old boy in the body of an eighteen-year-old man, his stature tall and solid with muscles hard from laboring beside his father in the fields. Lisa Pratt had lured him into her family home with a promise of popcorn and candy in front of their brand new color television set. Her parents had been at an evening revival meeting at White Cross Baptist Church. Jackson could have been right there in that living room with them for all Graye could remember. Lisa's brazen antics and the sexual encounter that ensued were all that now stood out in his memory.

He'd only been momentarily startled by her seductive overtures as she'd slowly stripped out of the floral print dress she wore, her very developed form blocking his view of *Mork and Mindy* on the 26" Magnavox console and cabinet purchased from Sears, Roebuck, and Company. He remembered how pale her complexion was in comparison to his own, the milky flesh tinged a vibrant shade of pink from the girl's own anxiousness. In that moment he had likened them both to the white and black crayons in a Crayola box.

His own nervousness had been quickly consumed by wanting, every muscle in his body hardening with obvious desire. And then they'd both been naked, the television abandoned for a full twenty minutes as they'd explored every square inch of each other's body. The moment could have gotten him shot had Mr. Pratt or his wife come home early, but they hadn't, and afterwards he'd gone back too many times to count to watch television with Lisa when no one else had been home.

As Angelette stripped slowly out of her traveling clothes he was reminded of that first time with Lisa. With each piece of clothing that fell to the floor he was taken back to a time and place when nothing else mattered but the length of rock hard maleness that strained eagerly against his slacks, and a girl who'd been available and willing to service his needs. But as he watched Angelette, there was no eagerness in her eyes. There was nothing about her posture or her expression that craved or needed him. Nothing about her that called out for him. There was no love in the look she tossed him, her gaze more a blend of disgust and annoyance. Her stare was cold and the chill was pervasive as it crept into the pit of his stomach and sickened him. The moment was nothing like that first time and so he thought of Lisa and the long list of women who'd come willingly after her, the memories warming his spirit.

Graye continued to stare after Angelette as she moved toward the bathroom, pausing for just a split second in the doorway before she shut herself inside. The sound of the lock being secured broke through his moment of reverie and as he listened to her moving behind the closed door, humming softly to herself, he suddenly wished he were fourteen again, his body erupting in orgasm as Mork from Ork chimed *Na No, Na No!* in the background.

Lifting his body from his seat there was a part of him that wanted to storm past the barrier she'd set between them. It would have been easy to barge through the enclosure to take what he wanted. He could have done that and been well with his decision, but as quickly as the thought had come to him, he couldn't summon the energy to fully contemplate the notion. Reaching for his jacket he eased his way out the front door and across the yard.

Things were different and nothing between them had changed. Angelette had barely spoken two words to him since she'd stepped out of the taxi. She'd refused to meet his gaze with her own as they sat listening to his grandmother and his mother bicker nonsensically back and forth. And when he'd clasped her hand beneath his own, to lead her back to their home, her legs had been like lead weights, dragging heavily behind him as she'd followed obediently.

As he walked aimlessly toward the center of town he pulled a Marlboro cigarette into his hands and lit it, pausing just briefly to stare at the flicker of flame that danced from the tip of his Bic lighter. Puffs of acrid smoke billowed into his face and up his nostrils as he toked on the end of the paper-wrapped cylinder. He was suddenly too tired to be contentious.

As he made his way to the door of the Easy-Slide Cafe resolve shouldered Graye's spirit. He'd had enough. He was too tired of wanting a woman who clearly didn't want him. He'd watched his father lose his soul with want of his mother. He'd seen it cripple the man, leaving him empty and hopeless with hurt and anger. Only his mother had survived, her and old Doc Burton carrying on as if his father had never lived and breathed every moment of his life for her. His father's love for Miss Jen Pearl had made the man crazy and Graye had walked far too many miles in his old man's shoes to go another step further.

He didn't want to go out like that, like his father, lost in a hell of his own making. His own soul was still up for grabs and he wasn't ready to let it go. As he pushed his way inside the dimlit nightclub, he no longer wanted to think of Angelette. The whisper of Jack Daniel's was the only thought he wanted on his mind.

TWENTY-SIX

Miss Jen Pearl quietly eased the door to Nana Leah's bedroom open to peer inside. The old woman lay curled on her right side, sleeping soundly, her breath blowing in loud gusts over her rose-colored lips. The room smelled sour, a rank mixture of dried urine and Bengay. The woman's clothes, both clean and dirty, were scattered in awkward piles across the dresser tops and the floor, and plastic grocery bags of heaven knew what lay in a neat pile by her bedside. It would need a good cleaning tomorrow, Miss Jen Pearl thought as she slowly closed the door and tiptoed her way back down the narrow hallway.

As she slipped into her own room, pulling her door shut behind her, her gaze met his and they both smiled, nervous tension spilling out in hushed giggles to fill the short expanse of space between them. Doc Burton had already shed his clothes, his camel-colored linen suit and starched white shirt folded neatly over the top of the cedar chest that sat at the foot of her bed.

Jen Pearl had imagined that moment more times than she cared to acknowledge. She had wanted

Horace Burton since forever. Everyone around them would have frowned on such a union. It also hadn't helped that both had been married to other people. It would have been well, fine, and good if Horace Burton had simply bedded her, keeping her a dirty little secret hidden from the public, but he had wanted more from her and she from him. Horace would have gladly laid claim to his love for her, sharing it with the whole world and ignoring what anyone else might have thought. But Jen Pearl would never have risked the safety of her children for anyone or anything and her children would have suffered most from their indiscretion.

The man sat upright against the headboard, his body braced by a mountain of pillows behind his balding head. His bare chest was exposed, the pale flesh peppered with a hint of snow white curls. He was thin, almost fragile in appearance and Miss Jen Pearl imagined that he might actually break if she were to hold him too hard. The thought was suddenly disconcerting and it showed on her face, her expression suddenly tensing.

"What's wrong, Jen Pearl?" he asked, concern rising in his tone.

She shook her head, pulling at the narrow belt holding her satin bathrobe closed. "I don't know what we was thinking," she whispered, her head waving from side to side.

The man smiled, reaching his arms out toward her. Miss Jen Pearl hesitated, then slowly made her way to the bedside, allowing him to wrap his thin arms around her and pull her down to sit beside him.

You worry too much. You want me here as much as I want to be here. That's all that matters," he whispered back, allowing his mouth to lightly graze her cheek.

His touch was electric, inciting the first flames of a raging fire beneath her. Miss Jen Pearl could feel her blood stirring in her veins, the sanguine fluid warming quickly as it pulsed from one end of her body to the other. Her breathing became heavy, her lips parting ever so slightly as she concentrated on the expanse of fingers that danced across her back and down the length of her arms. Heat spread from one end of her body to the other, disseminating until it peaked and warmed that spot between her thighs.

"I declare, Horace," she muttered softly. "You and I are too old for this nonsense."

The man laughed, the wealth of it rising from his midsection and bubbling warmly against the line of her neck up to tickle the curve of her ear lobe. He gently covered her face, mouth, and neck with warm, easy kisses. His tone was soothing, washing over her like balm as he whispered words of love, cooing them over and over again as if they were a prayer.

Outside, a full moon glistened brightly in a star filled sky. It shimmered with approval, casting a vibrant glow downward as it brightened the landscape. Just a hint of moonlight peeked through the blinds of Miss Jen Pearl's bedroom. It seeped through the window, across the floor, and brightened their bodies, as she and Horace Burton lay sprawled across the bedsheets. Miss Jen Pearl smiled and imagined that the man in the moon was getting himself quite an eyeful.

When Jack Daniel's was at its best, it empowered Graye to talk to dead men. Not any dead men he didn't know, but dead men who had meant the most to him when they'd been alive.

His father's intonations had always been the loudest, Otis' cold breath blowing foul over his son's numb body as Graye sat lost in the waste of his drunken stupor. His father had encouraged him, had motivated his actions, sending Graye down a path of no return. Graye had trusted him, believing that his father did know best, even if it was only his decaying corpse that spoke for him.

His father's ghost had faded substantially since Tate had come forth, light blinding all else around his lifeless form. That first time Graye had been afraid as Tate stood staring down at him, Graye's aching body framed by the dark grass in his mother's front lawn, a plastic tulip caught in the lacings of his track shoes. But Tate had simply smiled, extending his hand to pull Graye to his feet so he could sit comfortably against the steps of his mother's home.

Graye had been afraid at first, but Tate had held no grudges. Tate had been as he'd always been, at his best, goodness guiding his way. And he had shown Graye that things could be different if he wanted it so. Graye could be different and Graye had chosen to believe his best friend.

Tate had come without Jack Daniel's and had stood at Graye's side. He'd kept his promise to watch Graye's back and had helped Graye walk away from doing Angelette harm. But as quickly as he appeared, he'd been gone again and Graye desperately needed Jack Daniel's to bring his friend back to him. He needed Tate if he even wanted to think about his ever returning back home.

The bath water had grown cold as Angelette still lay beneath the wet blanket, her skin wrinkled into oblivion. She'd lost all sense of time, not knowing how long she'd been rocking back and forth against the porcelain tub, memories spinning like a panoramic movie through her mind.

"No more, no more, no more," she chanted softly, the words barely a whisper over her chattering lips. "No more, no more, no more," she chimed, the mantra reaffirming every thought, every opinion, and every facet of her existence as she suddenly saw it. She was through, wanting no more of the hurt and heartache that had been bequeathed to her. And mostly, wanting no more of Graye and everything he'd come to represent about herself, her life, and all she hated. "No more."

She'd heard him leave and had been thankful for it. But she knew he'd return and things would be as they'd been before. She shook the thought from her mind, pulling her crinkled fingers to her face as she splashed cool water over her eyes. "No more," she thought as she pulled her body upward, reaching for a thin towel that lay across the closed commode. "No more."

She stared at her reflection in the mirror, not recognizing the image that stared back at her. Who was this woman who'd come to claim her soul? Angelette recognized the desperation in the woman's eyes, the fear that painted the lines of her expression. Her fingers tapped against the glass, slapping at the red-tinged cheek staring back at her. "No more," she whispered, shaking her head from side to side.

Suddenly she could hear the ocean, the roar of the waves filling her ears. It washed away the rise of anxiety and calmed her nerves. She missed the sand, she thought, reminded of that moment her mother's words had blessed her with. She wondered if her mother had ever tasted the salted air as it filled her lungs. Curious to know if sand had ever scratched comfortably against her dark skin as the water kissed the crevices between her toes. Angelette remembered it all, the sand, and the salt, and the lull of the waves that called her name. She hoped her mother had been as blessed. Her gaze locked with the woman's in the mirror and the woman smiled. Understanding filled Angelette's heart. There would be no more.

A full bottle of spirits and two shot glasses sat in the center of the small table. Angelette sat alone, fingering the glass between her palms as she waited patiently for Graye to return. Inside she simmered, her anger having risen to a point of no return. It swelled thick and full, flooding through her bloodstream and seeping out of her pores. It carried a stench like spoiled milk, a foul odorous fume that seemed to permeate the air around her. The harshness of it was like nothing she'd ever experienced before.

Angelette couldn't begin to explain from where the fury had risen, not could she understand why its hold on her was so pervasive. But it had spread over her spirit, seeping into the minute crevices of her dreams and wishes, tainting everything that she was and had ever yearned to be. It lingered like acid in the hot tears that burned against the back of her eyelids and she imagined that if she could cry, the teardrops would scorch a heated path down her full cheeks.

Jack Daniel's sat full, the umber-colored fluid beckoning for her attention. This bottle was special, the first that she and Graye would ever share together. Angelette knew that time would soon bring him back home to her and Jack, and she was anxious for the moment when her anger and Jack Daniel's would fuel whatever was meant to be between her and Graye.

Graye stood outside the front door of the small cottage, uncertain whether or not he wanted to be home at all. He lingered in the midnight air, his hand wavering back and forth in front of the doorknob. He had sat for hours on a stool at the Easy-Slide Cafe, hoping that answers would have come to him by the time he reached the bottom of his bottle of scotch. But Tate had failed to show and not even the carcass of his father's memory had bothered to make an appearance. Graye couldn't remember when he'd last felt so alone.

Stepping through the front door he was surprised to see Angelette sitting in wait. He'd half expected her lifeless body to be curled against the bed they shared, her face to the wall as she clutched the edge of the mattress, the back of her head his only greeting. But Angelette was wide-eyed, anxiously waiting for him to return, a smile filling her sweet face.

"You still up?" Graye slurred softly, his words echoing through the quiet of the small room.

Angelette nodded her head, cocking it slightly to the side as she fluttered forest thick eyelashes in his direction. "Thought you and me could celebrate my coming home," she answered, gesturing toward the full bottle of Jack that called out from the table.

Graye nodded his head slowly, opening and closing his eyes as he struggled to focus. He laughed, the loud chortle ringing strangely through the air. "I'm already drunk, Baby Doll. Don't know if I can get any drunker!"

Angelette laughed with him. "Can't let me drink all by myself, Graye. What would that look like?" she asked coyly.

Graye stumbled the short distance to where she sat, dropping the weight of his body into the empty chair. As he did, Angelette twisted the cap off the liquor bottle and filled both glasses. She slid one in front of Graye, then lifted the second to her lips, the fluid burning across her tongue as she swallowed the shot in one gulp. She poured herself a second, then paused as her gaze met Graye's.

"Drink up, Graye. Can't be no party if you don't come on and join in."

Graye grinned as Jack Daniel's spilled over his fingers and into his mouth. He swiped at his lips with the back of his hand, then set the glass down so Angelette could refill it.

The small woman said nothing else as she poured drink after drink, pushing glass after glass into Graye's hands and her own. She could feel the heat of the bitter fluid flooding past her ire into her bloodstream, sharing space as if it and anger were old friends reunited. Angelette marveled at the sensation, her limbs slowly becoming numb and disjointed as if her head didn't belong to her body. Graye had been right about Jack having a mind of its own.

She didn't remember when she lifted the revolver from her lap. There had been no sensation in her palm and fingers as she had pressed her hand around the cold metal. Graye's eyes had widened only slightly when she'd cocked it, the click of the hammer registering somewhere in the dark, depths of his mind. And then he'd smiled, the gesture pulling at the muscles that creased his forehead and kept his face locked in a perpetual frown. He'd smiled, his drunken gaze glowing with joy. He'd smiled, mouthing the words *thank you,* and then Angelette emptied six rounds into his thick chest.

Angelette didn't remember how long she'd stood over his body. She stood watching him until the first rays of the morning sun had begun to peek through the curtained windows. Watching for any sign that Graye McAdams might stand back up and walk, making a fool of her and Jack both. But Graye never budged, his body sprawled over the kitchen table, the flow of his blood mixing with the alcohol that had spilled from the broken glass in his hand.

Angelette imagined that she had to be dreaming as she stared at the gun that lay on the floor at her feet. Her anger had gone cold, coagulating with

Graye's blood as it dripped like thick mud to the linoleum floor. She'd been surprised by the power of Jack Daniel's, the drink easing away ages of hurt and pain. She and Jack should have become friends sooner she thought as she exited the home, wanting to feel the morning rays against her skin.

Standing on the front porch she stared toward her mother-in-law's home, smiling as she watched old Doc Burton pulling his black sedan out of the driveway. She'd go see Miss Jen Pearl later she thought. She'd tell her what Jack had done. But first she had to make sure Graye wasn't coming back and so she waited at the top of the stairs. Waited to make sure Graye didn't get back up. Waited as the morning sun rained light down on the plastic gardens below.

EPILOGUE

On October thirteenth, almost nine years after the murder of Tate Butler, Angelette McAdams died from a lethal injection administered by a State of North Carolina Correctional Facility medical person. Sentence had been served for the murder of her husband, Graye McAdams.

Angelette had only asked for two things the night before: a slice of her mother-in-law's sweet potato pie and a shot of Jack Daniel's. They delivered the pie, but Jack had been denied. Angelette had thought this funny since Jack Daniel's had been the cause of all this commotion to begin with. Miss Jen Pearl had sent two pies, the bottom crusts coated with nuts and caramel just the way Angelette liked them.

Miss Jen Pearl had insisted on witnessing the young woman's death. "It's just something I need to do," she'd said quietly, "Just something I need to do."

Doctor Horace Butler sat at her side, his hand wrapped warmly over hers. They were older and grayer and still clinging to the fringes of love that had bound them together. Seeing them side by side had made Angelette smile, the warmth of it filling her heart.

In a rear seat in the back of the small witness room Miss Jen Pearl met her daughter-in-law's gaze and they both smiled. Blowing the old woman one last kiss Angelette nodded her head, understanding, and for the first time, in a long time, Miss Jen Pearl cried for the son who had been lost to her, and all the children she had loved and raised. She cried for the husband who'd done all that he thought he could, weeping for the love he'd given and the love he'd taken, for the dreams they'd not been able to share and the one's he'd not even known he could have.

Her tears fell like rain for the woman she'd found within herself, the person she'd come to like and understand. And then she cried for the child of her heart, the woman whose spirit had lingered where hers had been imprisoned until the day they'd tasted freedom, for just a brief minute, at the edge of an ocean, where the water had kissed the sand.

ACKNOWLEGEMENTS

Gratitude first, and foremost, to my Lord and Savior, for without his many blessings, none of this would be possible. I owe everything to a generous and loving God and I am grateful beyond measure.

There are no words to express how much I love doing what I do. From start to finish my literary journey has lifted me sky high and enabled me to soar. Writing is the air beneath my wings and with the sheer beauty of each word and every sentence and paragraph I've been able to go places I never imagined going.

Much love and appreciation to all those who have walked this path with me. To the family who continue to support me and love me, please know that I value each and every one of you.

And many thanks to new friends and old. All y'all know it is what it is and you just make me smile, smile, smile!

ABOUT THE AUTHOR

Writing for as long as she can remember, Deborah Fletcher Mello can't imagine herself doing anything else. Her first romance novel, *Take Me To Heart*, earned her a 2004 Romance Slam Jam nomination for Best New Author. In 2005 she received Book of the Year and Favorite Heroine nominations for her novel, *The Right Side of Love*, and in 2009 won a Romantic Times Reviewer's Choice Award for her ninth novel, *Tame A Wild Stallion*.

For Deborah, writing is as necessary as breathing and she firmly believes that if she could not write she would cease to exist. Weaving a story that leaves her audience feeling full and complete, as if they've just enjoyed an incredible meal, is the ultimate thrill for her. Born and raised in Connecticut, Deborah now maintains base camp in North Carolina, but considers home to be wherever the moment moves her.

For additional information on Deborah and her books, visit her at www.deborahmello.blogspot.com.